LOVE
MEMORY

A MEMOIR & A PRACTICE
FATIMAH SALLEH

A CERTAIN WORK PRESS
Durham, NC 27703

Copyright © 2023 by Fatimah Salleh
All rights reserved, including the right of reproduction in whole or in part in any form.

ISBN: 979-8-9885914-1-2 (Paperback)

Publisher's Cataloging-in-Publication Data
Names: Salleh, Fatimah S., author.
Title: Love memory : a memoir and a practice / by Fatimah S. Salleh.
Description: Includes bibliographical references.
Durham, NC: A Certain Work Press, 2023.
Identifiers: LCCN: 2023911535

Subjects: LCSH
1. Salleh, Fatimah S.
2. Love
3. Autobiographical memory
4. Memory
5. Interpersonal relations
6. BISAC BIOGRAPHY & AUTOBIOGRAPHY
7. Personal Memoirs
8. BODY, MIND & SPIRIT / General
9. FAMILY & RELATIONSHIPS / General

Classification: LCC BF575.L8 .S35 2023 | DDC 128/.46/092--dc23

Cover Design by Micah Sorensen and Rosie Gochnour Serago

Manufactured in the United States of America

"...FOR GOD IS LOVE."
– John 4:8

"LOVE SAVES US ONLY IF
WE WANT TO BE SAVED."
– bell hooks, *All About Love: New Visions*

CONTENTS

8	Preface
10	Introduction
17	718-474-6652
20	Being Beautifully Black
22	Poetry
24	A Mother's Access
27	Safe
29	Mom's Welcome Of Excitement
32	Platanos (Plantains)
34	Love Letters
38	No Translation Needed
42	Love Time
43	Race Standard Time (RST)
47	Baby Standard Time (BST)
50	Auntie
53	Dissertation Standard Time (DST)
57	Miscarriages And Holy Carried
61	Kingdom Calculus
65	Baked Macaroni
67	Not A Dog Person
71	Ginny's Final Words
76	Unicorn Stylz

78	Defiant Friendship
88	Uncle George
93	Pastoral Reassurance
95	Pastor People
97	An Unruly Spiritual Journey
100	Radical Welcome
105	Religious Refugee
109	White Women + Friendship
110	A Feminist Mormon Housewife
115	Bookwork + Trustwork
119	Organized Rebellion
125	Come Out And Stay In
128	Love Circle Roll Call
129	Faithful Family
131	Laughter
134	Anger Bearers
138	The *Whoop!* Wing Of The Love Circle
141	Grief Walkers
145	A Continuation, Not A Conclusion…
148	Afterword
150	About The Author

PREFACE

During one of our last rounds of edits before this book was to be published, I stalled returning it to my editor, Marci McPhee. The edits should have taken me no longer than an hour or two, but I could not get myself to sit at my computer and get it done. After fifteen days with absolutely no progress on the latest revision, I penned an email to my editor, feeling like I owed her an explanation for my delay:

> Good morning Marci,
> …I got scared. I am scared to finish the book as the time draws nearer to the finish. I had no idea until now just how hard it has been for me to do these last final edits. For my delay, I apologize. I am pulling myself together, as my Nana used to say, and it will be done.

Marci's response:

> No apologies needed. In the book we've got love time, baby time, dissertation time. For writing time, you take all the time you need, I say. No deadline as far as I'm concerned.

And this work is scary and vulnerable, no question. At the same time, you've done a beautiful job of painting yourself in an honest light, neither pure saint nor sinner, but an endearing blend, like us all. Very relatable, and so helpful. I think often of your insights that have helped me, and can't wait for others to be blessed by your honest words... in God's time.

Carry on, whenever you are ready, faithful Fatimah.

It is no easy feat for a woman of color to offer a part of herself — her writing and her memories — into a world that habitually disrespects and dismisses our bodies and our stories. I know releasing my love memories into the world opens me up to both the beauty and the cruelty of this world. It is this cruelty that makes me flinch and stall. This little book asked me to build my bravery.

The Spirit, with its penchant for nudging me out of hiding; add to that, my love circle who remain catalysts of courage; an editor like Marci; and you finally finish the little book with big memories. Despite the world. Because of the world. For the world.

And that is how this preface is about the finish.

INTRODUCTION

At the end of 2022, I finished a series of speaking engagements in Utah and I was tired of hearing myself talk. After hours of public speaking and preaching, I didn't know what I really wanted to say anymore, or if I had said all I needed to say.

After giving it some thought, I was tired. Tired of directing my conversation with God, always seemingly choosing the pressing topic of the hour and asking for specific guidance about a certain problem, or inspiration for a particular scripture. I did not want to do that anymore. I wanted more conversations with God where I wasn't leading. Not that God wasn't answering my prayers, but I felt that my voice had taken over the conversations. I wanted God to speak to me when God wanted, on whatever God wanted to talk about.

I yearned for the time to wait on listening, to come back to myself and hear the Divine within me. I needed to take a small hiatus from my self-directed divine dialogue. Step back from preaching and teaching. So, I decided to be quiet — a holy hush.

I began this practice of holy hush by telling those around me that I would not be accepting any preaching, speaking, or teaching assignments for the next little while. I was honest with them about both my fatigue and my season of wander and wonder.

As it turns out, God is loquacious. It seems that when I got quiet and started listening, I could hear God's running dialogue with me.

Within the first few days of relative self-quiet, I fasted and prayed that I could hear God with more clarity and understand what seemed to be the new twists and turns of my call. Pretty quickly, I began to be flooded with what I now affectionately call "love memories." Memories of all the ways I experience an abundance of love.

It looks like Holy Spirit wanted me to begin at remembering. It is profound to me that the Holy Spirit is described both as a comforter and one that helps us remember.[1] God sends us a divine memory aide. When God got to talking to me, it was in memories.

Many seasons ago, I received a blessing that quoted Luke 12:48: "Where much is given, much is required." This line always made me uneasy, because I felt it overwhelming to think about what could be required of me. Yet here I am now pondering, "What if what I have been given is love?" If this is the case, then according to the scripture, I am required to move in love in the ways it has been abundantly bestowed upon me.

1. "But the *Comforter*, which is the Holy Ghost, whom the Father will send in my name, he shall teach you all things, and bring all things to your *remembrance*, whatsoever I have said unto you" (John 14:26, emphasis added).

This book is simple. It is an account, my account of love and being loved. And, in turn, what love doth require of me.

By writing this book, sitting in my love memories, I slowly developed a practice that allowed me to sink into the memories, the work of love memory. First, I tried to make myself present to the memory. I did that by imagining questions around my five senses — what did love taste, smell, feel, sound, and look like? Then, as I allowed the memory to settle, my soul traveled back. Look for the workbook/journal to accompany this book, offering a deeper dive into the details of this practice, and inviting you to join me on this journey of reflection into your own memory.

As you read this book, you will find some memories sound and read different than others. For so many of these memories, if the person in the memory was still living, I contacted them, first, for permission and second, to see if they remembered things the way I did. We almost always never remembered the same moments. In fact, this part of the practice — reaching out to a fellow memory bearer, is what I call memoryscape. And it was one of the biggest blessings and surprises of this project.

Memoryscape is a living memory work, where an experience is shared. Together, with a fellow memory bearer, you travel back and simultaneously fill in the memory for each another. Memoryscaping with loved ones allowed me the additional opportunity to express gratitude for those who have walked well with me, those who have diligently taught me about love and held me in the best of ways.

For some of these stories I share, my fellow memory bearer is gone. I could not call them up, hear their voice, nor relish in the shared memories. For those stories, the reader may notice that there is a different feel to the writing and reflection, perhaps less color and contrast. People hold memory with us and sometimes they even hold the memory *for* us. When our memory bearers transition, that memory goes with them. Sometimes you find that you are the only one left holding that memory and while I cherish it, it is not the same feeling as the collective or shared memory. I discovered that part of my grief for that person was that I was the only one holding our shared memories. Especially when I am all that is left of that memory, I am so deeply grateful to hold these memories close and have the privilege to record them.

These love memories built me. They contain some of the greatest people I have had the blessing to know. I am truly the product of a good love.

At the end of most of my vignettes, I hold up a phrase which allows me to complete this practice. It loosely follows that scriptural text, "for where much is given, much is required." Indeed, because I am given so much love, much love is required of me. Below is the remix to that scripture, composed in rhythm to the work of my love memory.

LOVE SHOWED UP AS _____ AND SHOWERED ME IN _____. AS A RECIPIENT OF THIS ACT OF LOVE

ABUNDANT, I COMMIT TO _____.

718-474-6652

AS THE FIRSTBORN, I was a premature baby, arriving into the world at five pounds, five ounces. Within 24 hours of my birth, I was diagnosed with spinal meningitis (an infection on the covering of the spine). The doctors at Kings County Hospital in Brooklyn, New York gave me a slim chance of surviving the infection.

As the story is told to me, I was taken home from the hospital a few weeks later, still not fully thriving. My Mom decided to bring me to my father's mother, Nana. At the time, my grandmother was a "baby nurse." She went into rich, mostly white families and helped them with their newborn babies. I grew up seeing a pantheon of our family pictures on Nana's dresser with an occasional spattering of white children in the mix that she had helped raise. So it is no surprise that my mother thought I needed my grandmother's care. It is both my mother's and Nana's testament that I flourished under the additional care of my Nana. Her care, in all the gazillion ways it showed up, is why I still flourish and thrive.

I think my relationship with Nana was always tethered to my life. She would swoop in at various seasons of my life and take care of me/us. When my Mom went to medical school, Nana helped take care of me and my three younger siblings. When we moved from New York to Utah, my Mom flew my Nana out at least yearly to spend time with all of us. The love between my Mom and my Nana is another subject for another day. Suffice it to say, it was lovely.

I was young when I started calling Nana on the phone. I memorized her number before I was ten years old. I talked to her every week, sometimes multiple times a week, until she passed away on March 1, 2021, three weeks before her 97th birthday. Hers is the first phone number I committed to memory. Over her life she had multiple other phone numbers, but this is the phone number I remember, some forty years later. This is the phone number of my youth.

I remember Nana always picking up the phone to talk to me. No matter the hour or the day. Oh, I am sure there were times where she was not available and she called me back, but that is not my memory. The memory is Nana always answering the phone for me.

Sometimes I called early in the morning or late in the evening. I always started the conversation with, "Hi, Nana. Whatcha doing?" And she always replied, "What is any sane person doing at this hour?" I giggled, knowing it was a rhetorical question, and quickly dove into the story of the day.

I often argued with my mother, especially in the years following my parents' divorce. I routinely called my Nana to tell her all the ways I was wronged by my mother. Somehow, someway, my grandmother helped me try to understand my mother and reevaluate my words and actions. She often said to me, "Now, Timah, why would you go and say something like that?" Also a rhetorical question.

I regularly apologized to my Mom after a talk with Nana. You would think I could pick up the trend after a few years, but nothing deterred me from seeking out my Nana's wisdom, even if it often sided with my mama. Even though I had to do a lot of apologizing and learning, I knew Nana was right. She had a way of teaching me hard lessons that called me to repentance, yet simultaneously landed me in grace and love. It got to the point that if I disagreed with my Mom, she would tell me to call my grandmother.

Towards the end of Nana's life, she would say at the end of our conversations, "Thank you for calling."

No, Nana. Thank you. Thank you for a lifetime of answered calls.

LOVE SHOWED UP AS ANSWERED PHONE CALLS AND SHOWERED ME IN WISDOM. AS A RECIPIENT OF THIS ACT OF LOVE ABUNDANT, I COMMIT TO SHOWING A LOVE THAT WILL ANSWER THE CALL.

BEING BEAUTIFULLY BLACK

MY FATHER IS A LOT OF THINGS. He certainly is a complicated figure in my life. Yet one thing remained uncomplicated: his love of Blackness. I grew up regularly hearing him extol the features of Black people. He told us our noses were wide and therefore we could breathe better. Our lips were full and that made us better to kiss. Our hair was curly and that offered more protection from the sun. Our skin was dark and that was beautiful. This was on repeat throughout the years my mother stayed married to him and we lived together. I grew up hearing this dialogue so frequently that it often made me giggle and roll my eyes.

    I had no idea why my father felt the need to keep telling us these things about our physical features. At the time it seemed silly. I did not realize until I was older, far into my adulthood, that I had never looked in the mirror and hated my Blackness. I, a Brown/Black woman, who would eventually be surrounded in whiteness, never looked in the mirror and wished I wasn't Black. I came of age in America, where the features of Black bodies are rarely extolled outside of athleticism and as a means of commodification. Yet, I have never regretted the ways in which Blackness shows itself on my body. This is perhaps one of the most profound gifts my father bestowed on me.

LOVE SHOWED UP AS <u>PRONOUNCEMENTS OF BLACK BEAUTY</u> AND SHOWERED ME IN <u>SELF-LOVE</u>. AS A RECIPIENT OF THIS ACT OF LOVE ABUNDANT, I COMMIT TO SHOWING A LOVE THAT <u>DEFIES THE DOMINANT RACIST AESTHETIC.</u>

POETRY

YEARS LATER, WHEN MY SON was in the seventh grade, Xavier wrote me a poem and penned it on a T-shirt. I have never worn or washed the T-shirt, afraid that his words, written in red, blue, and green, would disappear. It is quite something to receive a gift of poetry, and even more so when it's written by your adolescent teenager. I keep this T-shirt on the left-hand side of my top dresser drawer. I know exactly where to find it when I need to read his words. I offer you a few lines:

> *You always stayed true to you.*
> *You gave us from clothing to shoes.*
> *Never were you hard back.*
> *You taught us what it means to be Black.*
> *You went through labor over and over again.*
> *You taught us what it means to grow up living as Black men.*
>
> *I cannot pay you back for everything you did.*
> *I still can't believe you had four kids.*
> *You are amazing for the things you did.*

LOVE SHOWED UP AS <u>POETRY</u> AND SHOWERED ME IN <u>A CHILD'S RECOGNITION</u>. AS A RECIPIENT OF THIS ACT OF LOVE ABUNDANT, I COMMIT TO SHOWING A LOVE THAT <u>WRITES</u>.

A MOTHER'S ACCESS

SHORTLY AFTER MY MOTHER gathered all seven of us and fled my father in New York, she started working in the emergency room at a local hospital in Brownsville, Texas. Her 24-hours shifts were brutal, both for her and for us kids. Though we had a wonderful woman who stayed with us when Mom was working, there was no doubt that my mom's absence was keenly felt. And while we had someone to watch over us, I dare not tell the stories of how many nannies we ran off because of how difficult it was to care for all of us. I am sure this was just another stressor for Mom; having anyone want to stay with us for any prolonged period of time was part of the trial. One nanny met my Mom in the driveway with her bags packed, after one day with us. Post-divorce my Mom made professional decisions knowing that she was essentially our only parent, certainly our only caregiver. Throughout my mother's demanding career as a family medicine doctor, she continually and intentionally made pathways for us to have as much access to her as possible.

In the ER, unless she was in the midst of caring for a life-and-death situation, we could talk to her whenever we called. She let the front desk personnel know that whenever we called, we were to be patched through. The amazing front desk folks got to know us so well that they could recognize our voices and knew our names, and we got to know them and their names too. It also goes to show that we were a needy bunch and probably called far too often. My youngest sister called to complain that everyone ate all the "good" popsicles and left the nasty purple ones, and yes, we teased her about it.

We called Mom to have her settle disputes, remind us of chore assignments, listen to our day, and also hear about what forms she would have to sign when she got home. We called about the mundane and the big. Quite a few times she said, "That is something I will deal with when I get home." When she did get home, she was often so tired that she asked us to remind her what our punishment was or what agreement she had made. Due to her fatigue, she often forgot about grounding us, and we were happy to let her forget.

Yes, sometimes she couldn't answer, but Mom always called us back. I think part of us knew that she had a demanding, life-saving profession but sometimes we called just because we could, just because she was available to us, and we missed her. So, yes, we called about popsicles, who got to watch their TV program first, and who wasn't doing their part. All the while my Mom listened, doled out correction, advice, and care.

When we moved to Utah in the summer of 1991, my mother left her work in the ER to join a clinic. She asked to work "mother's hours," 7:30 a.m. - 3:30 p.m. With this schedule, she could see most of us off to school and be home close to when we got home. The clinic normally ran on a 9-5 schedule and was reluctant to engage my mother's request due to logistics and staffing. My Mom kept pushing and found a way to start and end her clinical hours earlier to suit our school schedule.

Having a mother whose profession was vital and important, and yet could make us feel just as vital and important, deeply impacted my own motherhood and sense of belonging. I learned early that while my Mom could not be physically present, she was reachable. I learned that despite all the hard stuff my mother was doing every day in her chosen career, my adolescent needs, complaints, and story sharing always had a pathway to be heard. My mother moved institutions, protocols, and work culture to continually offer us access to her. My mother took measures to nudge and bend her career to center us.

LOVE SHOWED UP AS <u>UNPRECEDENTED ACCESS</u> AND SHOWERED ME IN <u>MY MOTHER'S GOODNESS.</u> AS A RECIPIENT OF THIS ACT OF LOVE ABUNDANT, I COMMIT TO SHOWING A LOVE THAT <u>BENDS SOCIETY'S NOTIONS OF ACCESS IN AN EFFORT TO BE PRESENT WHERE I AM MOST NEEDED.</u>

SAFE

SEVERAL DAYS AFTER MY PEERS at Davis High School elected me homecoming queen, our principal called me into his office. It seems that there were numerous complaints that a Black girl was the school's homecoming queen in Kaysville, Utah. He asked whether I still wanted to go through town in a convertible at the homecoming parade, or step down due to the calls. He wanted to know if I felt safe, considering the upset of some within our community.

I chose to continue. The ride through town scared me. I was fortunate to have two great classmates with me in the vehicle, who were also part of the homecoming party.

My mother ran beside the car through the whole parade, just to ensure my safety. At one point, I told her she could go, I thought I would be okay. She refused to leave me.

Nothing happened during that homecoming parade. By all accounts it was uneventful, and everything went as planned. Yet I knew something grand and deeply eventful. I knew my Mom would run beside a slow-moving car for blocks, just to make sure I was safe. And I was safe. Safe to be a Black/Brown homecoming queen in a 98% white school, white neighborhood, and white town.

LOVE SHOWED UP AS <u>PRESENCE</u> AND SHOWERED ME IN <u>SAFETY</u>. AS A RECIPIENT OF THIS ACT OF LOVE ABUNDANT, I COMMIT TO SHOWING A LOVE THAT <u>PUTS MY BODY IN UNSAFE PLACES TO ENSURE THE SAFETY OF OTHERS.</u>

MOM'S WELCOME OF EXCITEMENT

I WENT TO UNDERGRADUATE SCHOOL in Logan, Utah, about an hour away from home. While I had applied to multiple schools out of state, Utah State University offered me a four-year Presidential Leadership scholarship that was incomparable to anything else I received. This sizeable scholarship went to only a few individuals across the state, typically one leader in any given high school. My eventual acceptance of this award caused an immediate backlash from the parents of my high school peers. So much so that the Director of Admissions called me to say that in all his years of awarding this scholarship he had never seen such vitriol and racism.

I was deeply hurt but unsurprised. I had been here before. And this is why I wanted to leave Utah. Even though I did only two years of high school in the state, I was done being one of two Black/Brown[1] girls (the other being my sister) in a school of almost 2,000 students. It was the reason I applied to only one Utah college. I wanted to get away from the specific type of racism honed in the mountains of Utah — a sort of pseudo-benevolent, passive, dirty racism.

This is why I came home from college almost every

weekend. As soon as classes were over on Friday, I headed back home.

I could always depend on one thing when I arrived home: my mother would be excited to see me. My Mom has this ability to show such excitement that you can't help but feel so deeply loved. It doesn't matter if you have been gone for seven days or seven hours; she was happy you came in through the door.

Utah State University was a predominantly white school, boasting about 5% African Americans in the student body. In a time where I felt different and got tired of standing out, coming home was an exhale. My mother's excitement, the inhale. It is something to be met with excitement. My Mom's enthusiasm over my presence taught me what it was to feel love jubilant. Oh, how I needed to feel every bit of her bold and full reception of me, every single time. It never got old. It will never get old. It is what my heart came to expect of her love. Her excitement was my safe landing in an unsure time. I could not be more grateful to have been shown this type of love when I needed it most.

I recall the scripture relaying the parable of the prodigal son.[2] One of the amazing parts of this story is the father's excitement at seeing his son come home. This father runs to meet his son — not only to meet his son but to hug and hold him.

It is something deeply moving to be loved in a way that your entrance fosters unabashed excitement.

LOVE SHOWED UP AS <u>EXCITEMENT</u> AND SHOWERED ME IN <u>ENTHUSIASM</u>. AS A RECIPIENT OF THIS ACT OF LOVE ABUNDANT, I COMMIT TO SHOWING AN <u>EXCITED LOVE</u>.

---

1. This book references AP guidelines in referring to racial categories. See David Bauder, "AP says it will capitalize Black but not white," *AP News*, July 20, 2020. Also see Erin Goulding, "Opinion: The decision to capitalize Black and not white," *BYU Daily Universe*, August 4, 2020.
2. Luke 15:11-13.

PLATANOS (PLANTAINS)

PUERTO RICANS, LIKE A LOT OF CARIBBEAN FOLKS, have a simple way of frying a fruit called plantains (platanos — like a starchy banana). I grew up with my Mom making plantains and there was never enough to go around. Probably because there were so many of us and we all loved them so much that my Mom would have to be frying plantains all day. It has and continues to be a comfort food for me.

My husband Eric had never tasted plantains before he came into our family, and he immediately liked them. He started watching how my Mom made them, everything from how she picked them out at the grocery store to how she thinly sliced them at an angle in preparation for the shallow fry.

During many hard days, my husband presented me with a whole plate of perfectly prepared Puerto Rican platanos. Here my Danish-Scottish-English husband took the time to make me one of my favorite cultural comfort foods. One particular morning, I had been up for hours and had forgotten to eat. Silently and gently, my husband came up to me and placed the platanos on my desk and simply said, "Eat." I could have cried. This was just one of the many times he prepared food, just for me, as a great act of care.

LOVE SHOWED UP AS <u>PLATANOS</u> AND SHOWERED ME IN <u>PHYSICAL CARE</u>. AS A RECIPIENT OF THIS ACT OF LOVE ABUNDANT, I COMMIT TO SHOWING A LOVE THAT <u>PROVIDES MEALS THAT OFFER COMFORT AND SEE TO A PERSON'S PHYSICAL SUSTENANCE.</u>

LOVE LETTERS

"MOM, IS THIS YOUR HANDWRITING?" I asked, stunned. I had traveled across the world to become acquainted with my Malaysian heritage. Here I was in Kuala Lumpur holding a stack of yellowing letters from my grandfather in my mother's unmistakable handwriting. It made no sense.

I knew that my grandfather, Suihaili, took the identity papers of his uncle and left Malaysia when he was around nineteen years old, looking for opportunity and adventure. In New York City, he found work as a seaman on ships that sailed the world, which appeased his wanderlust. Even though his travels took him on voyages across the globe and back again, he never made it back home to Malaysia. There in New York City, my Malaysian grandfather married my Puerto Rican grandmother and it was there he would make his home when he was in port. They would have three children, my mother being the oldest daughter.

Like my mother, I too was born in New York City, just nine months after Suihaili's death. I have one old weathered picture of him and me, where I am snuggled in his arms.

Many years later, after my freshman year of college, at a certain point in my own journey of self-discovery, I realized I was well acquainted with my Black and Puerto Rican parts of my identity, but I knew little to nothing about my Malaysian side. It bothered me that there was a whole part of my ethnic identity that I proudly acknowledged but had yet to know deeper than just the naming.

I worked all summer and saved my money so I could afford a ticket to Malaysia. I asked my Mom if she would accompany me. She had been several times before, and understood my desire. While it was a big expense both financially and timewise, she said I had given her enough time to prepare for the multiple costs of the trip. After all these years, I don't know if that was necessarily true, but my Mom had this thought that she shared with us a few times and it stuck: "Most of us don't just have the extra money to travel, but still find a way to do it anyway. It is worth the sacrifice." I think she may have joined me on this pilgrimage of sorts because she believed in the intrinsic and spiritual value of traveling and heritage-seeking.

My grandfather's family, my grandfather's people are my family, my people. In a pleasant, spacious living room in Sibu, Sarawak, crowded with cousins, aunties, and uncles, my Malay relatives graciously shared their richly spiced food and their stories of my grandfather. At one moment in our hours' long conversation, someone brought out several boxes filled with letters. Loads of letters spanning decades, from my grandfather in New York, home from his most recent sea voyage, to his family in Malaysia.

They kept his letters. All of them. Even though he passed away more than twenty years ago. As my mother and I reverently started reading his letters, I quickly noticed that the letters were written in English and in my mother's handwriting.

"Mom, is this your handwriting?" I asked.

"Yes," she responded. "You have to remember your grandfather had a third-grade education and was basically illiterate. He asked me to write his letters for him. He didn't teach us Bahasa Malay so I wrote them in English."

I exhaled deeply. I imagined my Mom as a young woman, welcoming her traveling father home from the sea, pulling out paper and pen to take dictation for relatives back home. Those pages I now held in my hand had traveled across the world, then read aloud and translated at impromptu family gatherings. I imagined their pride in their Suihaili, making his way in the big world but never forgetting his people.

These letters, written in my mother's handwriting, spoke of my grandfather's love and how he hoped to return home to Malaysia to see all of them. Tears filled our eyes as my mother and I took turns reading portions of his letters out loud. Our surrounding family listened and wept with us as the letters were read aloud.

Unfortunately, he never returned home to Malaysia and died of esophageal cancer the year I was born. He was sixty years old.

LOVE SHOWED UP AS <u>KEEPSAKES</u> AND SHOWERED ME IN <u>THE WORDS OF MY ANCESTOR</u>. AS A RECIPIENT OF THIS ACT OF LOVE ABUNDANT, I COMMIT TO SHOWING A LOVE THAT <u>FINDS A WAY TO HOLD UNTO WORDS.</u>

NO TRANSLATION NEEDED

I WANT TO BE HONEST, I was not a good traveler on that trip to Malaysia. In fact, I was downright horrible in certain cases. I did not realize how hard it would be for me to travel such a long distance and embrace a culture so different from my own. In addition, I was not as willing to learn as I needed to be. I was not prepared for what this trip would demand of me. At one point in our journey, my mother said that if she was not so far away, she would go back home and leave me to finish the trip by myself. Yes, I was that bad.

On one such occasion of my assholishness (not a word, but definitely befitting my behavior), I refused to come out of my room to a large family dinner in honor of my mother and me, to meet the child and grandchild of Suhaili. The dinner, held in Sibu, a rural area in Sarawak, Malaysia, required some of the family to travel long distances, some even by boat. Relatives young and old traveled this distance to meet the "long lost relatives from America." As they arrived, I stayed holed up in a room, refusing to come out. I was tired and didn't understand the language and couldn't sit through another meal where I understood so little. I told Mom to go meet everyone without me. I would eat in my room; I didn't want to meet anyone else. My mother was mortified, rightly so.

Then a friend of the family came into my room, demanded that I get up and meet all the family who had traveled great distances to meet us. Not used to this friend using such a serious tone, I acquiesced. As soon as I entered the room, I was immediately greeted by so many people who had been patiently waiting for me to appear. I knew instantly that my attitude was deeply wrong. Older Malay women, my grandfather's siblings, nieces, and nephews, crowded me, speaking in Bahasa Malay. The only word I could make out was the name of my grandfather. His name was said through tears, smiles, and even laughter. My Malay family took turns hugging me and holding me, and I could not stop my tears from meeting theirs. We finally all ate, and I just listened as our family friend translated for me the shared tales of my grandfather. It was nothing short of an honor and privilege to meet my family and listen as they conjured memories of their beloved relative so that I might know the man they all knew and loved. There was a spirit to their memory-sharing with my mother and me. I got to know my grandfather I never knew, and they got to remember him in all his beauty with one another.

When the dinner finished, I stood and began hugging them goodbye. Although I could not understand Bahasa Malay and they could not understand English, we understood family. I was finally meeting the family that my grandfather never saw again. And here I stood, his granddaughter, finally able to receive the love my grandfather bestowed and transferred to me.

LOVE SHOWED UP AS <u>FINDING FAMILY</u> AND SHOWERED ME IN <u>EMBRACE</u>. AS A RECIPIENT OF THIS ACT OF LOVE ABUNDANT, I COMMIT TO SHOWING A LOVE THAT <u>TRANSCENDS LANGUAGE</u>.

FURTHER + MORE:

When we first arrived in Kuala Lumpur, Malaysia, we were greeted by a cousin of my grandfather, yet somehow, I was to call him Grandpa. They explained the Malaysian family naming structure, but in some ways, it was so different from my own American construct that I could not fully understand it. Yet, having never known my Grandpa Suhaili, I was thrilled to embrace this wonderful cousin of his as Grandpa Zaidi.

Zaidi, a WWII war hero and then Governor of Sarawak,[1] was our host when we arrived in Malaysia and he treated us with so much kindness and charity. One evening over dinner, (I do believe no conversation happens in that culture sans food), Zaidi decided to share his own story about my grandfather Suhaili.

---

1. Sarawak is one of the thirteen Malaysian states.

Zaidi was living abroad in London, England for his undergraduate education. Far from his homeland, family and friends, Zaidi was not only deeply lonely but poor and hungry. Serendipitously, Suhaili's ship had docked in England for a couple of days on business. The way Zaidi tells it, my grandfather sought him out, found him, got him something to eat, bought him a load of groceries, and also found time to take him to the movies. As Zaidi told us of this time, he cried. It appeared that none of the family around the table had heard this story.

Zaidi never saw my grandfather again to tell him what his visit had meant. Zaidi emphasized that welcoming my mother and me was part of him offering back some of the generosity he received so many years back.

LOVE TIME

LOVE TIME WOULD HAVE YOU fall in love with a baby you've just met.

Love time means that the days feel like years and the years like days sometimes. Especially when my children were toddlers.

Love time has you still feeling the love of a person even after they have transitioned on.

These love memories in this book are done in love time.

RACE STANDARD TIME (RST)

I HAVE TAUGHT ABOUT RACE AND RACISM for more than twenty years. Throughout my time as a Diversity, Inclusion and Equity (DEI) consultant and facilitator, I realized that time passed differently when teaching about my own humanity and the humanity of the dehumanized. The task of speaking about racism and other oppressive systems exacted a heavy tax on me — there was a cost enacted in the ever present work of engaging with these matters.

Time was just one of the costs. Around the time of Treyvon Martin's murder and the subsequent onslaught of Black death footage, I decided that teaching racism, while simultaneously living into its horrors and fears, created a different time continuum. This time system was based on how the work cost me.

My measure of race standard time (RST) was a 1:3 ratio. For every hour I sat in DEI teaching or training, it might translate into three hours of my life, due to the emotional, mental, and spiritual toll it exacted from me. This is what race standard time (RST) means to me. This ratio is dynamic. Two separate and moving experiences helped fortify my own depiction of this race standard time.

In 2018, I was facilitating a workshop on race education

with Vivette Jefferies-Logan in Pittsboro, North Carolina. A member of the Occoneechi Band of the Sipone Nation, Vivette and I had previously met on a few occasions before partnering for this workshop together. She is now, I am grateful to say, one of my dearest friends.

When we finished our first full day of training, she approached me. (I was tired, but this is how one always feels after teaching about oppression for hours.) The room was relatively cleared, and Vivette asked if she could offer a prayer over me in her native tongue, which would require her to lightly touch me. I readily agreed. She said, "The aura around you is hazy and heavy, you didn't come into this place like that. Whatever it is that people released unto you from this workshop, it is not yours to hold. You need to let it go. My prayer for you is to help release you from things you are holding from others that are not yours to bear." She prayed for me, right there, in her Indigenous tongue that I didn't understand but deeply felt. The fatigue did not pass but the weight of the fatigue did. I cried and profusely thanked her.

Fast forward several months. I was in Utah, more than halfway across the nation from my North Carolina home, preaching about social justice and the importance of wrestling with the issues of racism in Christianity, more specifically, within the tradition of The Church of Jesus Christ of Latter-day Saints (LDS). As a preacher, sometimes you have sermons where you know you have been a good enough instrument for the Spirit. In those cherished cases, a mighty work flows through the congregants, and they have personal encounters with the Divine. After these types of sermons, I often spend more time connecting with folks one on one than I ever did preaching at the pulpit. It is definitely a beautiful part of preaching: getting to engage and meet people as they personally share with you how God is moving in them.

On this specific occasion, a young woman waited until I had greeted and spoken to all those in line. Then she quietly approached me and said that her grandmother, a Ute elder, would like to pray for me. Immediately humbled, I again readily agreed and followed her to meet the beautiful Brown woman at the back of the chapel. Her grandmother told me that I was carrying too much, and she wanted to pray over me to help me let go and be clear. She then prayed for me. Right there at the back of the chapel, I received a sacred blessing from a Ute grandmother. In response, I did what I usually do — I cried and hugged her.

These two sacred and sweet experiences allowed me to more clearly see that the spiritual cost of my preaching and teaching is a real and tangible thing. Shortly after these two blessed encounters with Indigenous holy women, I decided I needed to address the promptings of their prayers. This, in part, is how race standard time started for me. I needed to address how my work wholly impacted my being.

One hour of working in race matters exacted far more than 60 minutes from me. And while I denote a 1:3 ratio, I am certain that at times it is even more than that. My soul knows it has cost me more than three hours to defend my own humanity, but this is the best I can think of as a measure — for now. It took blessings from these women to reckon with the toll it takes to look at an evil like racism, describe it, teach its historic harms, and offer — at times plead for — pathways of change. All the while living in the midst of those said harms. Every. Single. Day. Indeed, the laying on of hands from these two women even changed time itself.

LOVE SHOWED UP AS THE <u>BLESSINGS OF HOLY WOMEN</u> AND SHOWERED ME IN <u>REVELATION</u>. AS A RECIPIENT OF THIS ACT OF LOVE ABUNDANT, I COMMIT TO SHOWING A LOVE THAT <u>HEEDS THE BLESSING.</u>

BABY STANDARD TIME (BST)

MY FIRST CHILD, MICAH, was born in 2002 and my second, Xavier 23 months later in 2004. In less than two years I had two children. It was one of the hardest times in my life to care for both an infant and a toddler. One day Eric came home from graduate school and asked one question that immediately incurred my wrath, which surprised me. The question: "How was your day?" These four words grouped together in this order, posed as a question, met a quick death in our early parenting years from which it would never reemerge. It was in response to this question, before the moratorium, that I ranted to my husband that I spend my days covered in bodily fluids either from my own body or that of our children. I told him I simply craved a day where I was just dry. A day where I could sleep when I wanted to, not at the maniacal schedule of a 1-month-old. These were my lofty goals during this time.

Motherhood, especially when my children were babies and toddlers, required so much from me that while I was aware of time, it did not seem to be particularly friendly. In fact, I would say that me and baby standard time had an adversarial relationship. Every time I put my head down to rest, a baby cried. When I got on the phone to finally have an adult conversation, my toddler made some attempt to harm himself. I spent a lot of my babies' childhood trying to carve out time to take a shower, comb my hair, or even go to the bathroom without an eyewitness. All the while, everyone around me was telling me to enjoy this time because before you know it, it will all be over and I couldn't get these days back. I felt guilt for the desire for a fast forward, and yet, while extremely rough going at times, I also hope I drank in the moments that sealed my motherhood.

While there were moments (many moments) when I desperately wanted out of this motherhood gig, there were also brilliant flashes of baby love that I keep banked in a sacred repository. One such time, when the universe paused for me and mine, was when our third son, Ronin, learned to kiss. You know those baby kisses that have not yet puckered but entail a gaping mouth and gooey saliva. Ronin, of all my children, loved to shower me in his kisses (and I do mean shower). He would start with one wide-mouthed, almost toothless kiss, and then he would just keep kissing. Once I tried and counted around 18 consecutive kisses before I couldn't hold back my laughter any longer. His kisses on repeat were nearly a daily event for a few months. This child would ask me to pick him up for the pure purpose of his kissing onslaught. This encounter was an unmitigated joy for me every single time.

Baby standard time. It's a thing. It's a time that is both a contradiction and a cognitive dissonance. The days are like years and the years like days. You want it to both speed up and slow down. You want to skip over it and yet not miss it.

LOVE SHOWED UP AS <u>BABY STANDARD TIME</u> AND SHOWERED ME IN <u>KISSES AND SLEEP DEPRIVATION</u>. AS A RECIPIENT OF THIS ACT OF LOVE ABUNDANT, I COMMIT TO SHOWING A LOVE THAT <u>ALLOWS TIME TO BE COMPLICATED</u>.

AUNTIE

IT IS PROBABLY NOT HARD TO TELL that the first years of my motherhood were more than just an adjustment — more like a seismic shifting. A few months after Micah was born, I drove him around so he could fall asleep and ended up in a vacant parking lot, doing loops. As Micah finally quieted, I brought the car to a slow stop. I then called my Mom and sobbed as quietly as I could.

"I can't do this anymore, Mom. I feel like I haven't slept in days. Micah won't sleep. I just can't do this. I don't want any more days like this."

As my Mom listened, she doled out a few immediate helpful thoughts, and then sent me to my physician because she was pretty sure I was in the throes of post-partum depression. Soon after that conversation in the parking lot, I started an anti-depressant. I also worked out a schedule with wonderful mamas in university family housing, where we watched one another's children while the other mother got a break. We even took turns making family dinners for one another, so we didn't have to cook all the time. Medicine and mother friendships saved me in the early years with Micah and Xavier.

In 2005, we left our Utah collegiate community, and

our little family of four moved across the country, with no family nearby, so that I could pursue my doctoral degree at UNC-Chapel Hill. At this time Micah was 3 and Xavier was 1. By 2007, I was pregnant with our third son, Ronin. I had finished my course work and was now trying to pass my five comprehensive exams, defend my proposal, and then write my dissertation. Getting pregnant during this time was not the most convenient, but honestly, I don't think there is ever a convenient time to have a small human take over your body. Nor does this society make it easy or convenient to have a baby. In the midst of a PhD is as good a time as any. (This outlook seemed relatively normal because my Mom had five of her seven children before she finished her family practice medical residency.)

My sister, Najah, was living and working in Hawaii when I announced to our family that I was pregnant again. Because my family had witnessed my struggles with post-partum depression, my sister naturally asked me some good questions about my preparation for the mental and physical toll the baby would most likely have on me. She also worried about the limited support system I would have with no family around. She and I had many conversations about all the measures needed to ensure my postpartum wellness. A few days before I went into labor and one day before her birthday, Najah moved to North Carolina.

She moved! My sister left her work and life in Hawaii. She packed all her bags, stayed with us for a few months and then moved into her own apartment down the street, to be with me.

To be with me!

She did laundry. She held and rocked Ronin at all hours of the day and night. She ordered me to go back to bed to get some rest. She gently removed him from my lap when I was dozing off. My sister loved on Ronin so much that we had a running joke that I was just the surrogate and Najah was his mother. In return, he threw up and pooped on her. To this day, auntie and nephew, born 31 years and 1 day apart, are close.

So I took my medicine, got some rest, took more showers, and fell into the care of my sister.

LOVE SHOWED UP AS A SISTER'S RESCUE AND SHOWERED ME IN A MELDING OF MOTHERHOOD. AS A RECIPIENT OF THIS ACT OF LOVE ABUNDANT, I COMMIT TO SHOWING A LOVE THAT CROSSES LAND AND SEA TO MEET YOU IN YOUR TIME OF NEED.

DISSERTATION STANDARD TIME (DST)

DR. JANE BROWN, OR JANE as she asked to be called, started out as my advisor when I began my graduate program at UNC-Chapel Hill. To meet Jane is to know she is good people. Born in rural upstate to a Quaker farming family, she is full of wonder and deep care.

The first semester of my program, I failed a major course, Media Law. I was devastated. I had never failed a course before except for Tennis 101 in my sophomore undergrad year. (But hey, that course was way too early in the morning in the cold of Utah.) Jane called me to meet with her after winter break. I had all Christmas to mourn my failure. She told me that I would have to retake the course and if I did not pass it the second time, they would dismiss me from the program.

I simply told her that they could kick me out of the program now because I was not taking that class again. I expressed my loathing of the class and the type of writing it demanded of me. I sat defiantly in her office chair and repeated my refusal to take Media Law again. Jane let me have my say and then she calmly looked at me and said, "You will take the course again and you will pass."

"No, I will not. That course is ridiculous and why is it even a requirement?!?!" I interrupted.

Jane continued, "You will take the class again and you will pass. Now, if you need a moment to scream, shout, and be angry, we can go outside right now, and I will scream with you. Then you will come back inside and retake this course."

I retook the course and passed. Jane found out my grade before it was posted, then called me to her office to cheer with me.

My doctoral degree was designed to be a three-year program: two years of fulltime course work and one year to write the dissertation. It took me seven years. The beginning of my third year in the program, when I was supposed to be taking comprehensive exams and writing my dissertation, I got pregnant with Ronin. The all-day sickness (not just morning sickness) was so bad my first trimester that I was hospitalized due to dehydration. When I told Jane I was pregnant, she said I was one of the first students that she could remember to be pregnant while doing this degree. She then told me that our society never makes it easy or convenient to have a child. She heard me out as I told her my best laid plans to finish writing my dissertation while I simultaneously grew a human in my body.

In fact, three months after having Ronin, I asked Jane for a meeting so we could go over my work. All I remember of this meeting was her reviewing my research and my theoretical framework and I truly did not understand a word that was coming out of her mouth.

My confusion must have shown all over my face because Jane stopped talking and simply said, "Are you getting any sleep?"

"Not really."

"Don't worry about any of this work right now. Go home and take care of yourself and Ronin. Your work will be here when the fog of motherhood clears."

I did not come back to her for another year.

When I returned, Jane was there. I started writing again. I defended my proposal and was now ABD (All But Dissertation). I started writing my first chapters. Let me be honest: Jane threw out my first 45 pages. From then on I had to write only in five-page increments until she was certain I knew what I was doing. She edited my work over and over again. She was meticulous, brilliant, and so deeply committed to seeing me finish and finish well.

While writing my last two chapters, I got pregnant with Zora. That baby was so unplanned that I thought it was the writing that was making me vomit. I loathed to tell Jane that I was pregnant again, especially when I was so close to finishing. When I finally did call her, she congratulated me, took a deep breath, and said, "Let's try to deliver this dissertation before the baby, okay?"

"Okay," I said.

That didn't happen.

I gave birth to Zora in February and called Jane from the hospital. She was so excited and came to visit me and meet the newest member of the family. While rocking our newborn, Jane told me she had finished another round of edits. "You will finish this, Fatimah. You will have two big deliveries this year, but nothing will compare to this little one."

Three months and a few more major edits later, I defended my dissertation with Zora in my lap and Dr. Jane Brown with me, there every step of the way. I was one of the last dissertations she would chair. She retired that same year, but not before she helped me cross one of the hardest finishing lines of my career.

LOVE SHOWED UP AS <u>A PROFESSOR'S CARE</u> AND SHOWERED ME IN <u>CONTINUAL SUPPORT</u>. AS A RECIPIENT OF THIS ACT OF LOVE ABUNDANT, I COMMIT TO SHOWING A LOVE THAT <u>HELPS YOU DO HARD THINGS.</u>

MISCARRIAGES AND HOLY CARRIED

IN MID-APRIL OF 2015, I suffered my second miscarriage, after my four children. Unlike my first miscarriage, my body wanted to hold on to this baby. Because of my body's refusal to let go of this nearly three-month-old fetus, my doctor strongly recommended a D and C (dilation and curettage). For all intents and purposes, my body was fully nurturing a child with no heartbeat.

That early spring had already seen a bevy of challenges. On April 1, Eric was practicing jiujitsu and through some weird accident had managed to blow out both his knees. While in the ambulance, the jiu-jitsu instructor called me to let me know that my husband had injured himself and was on his way to the hospital. I thought it was an April's Fool joke his friends were trying to play on me. It wasn't. Eric had a torn quadricep tendon in one knee and a torn patella tendon in the other. Both knees would undergo immediate surgery. Eric would have weeks of immobility since both legs would be in straight braces with no movement. His recovery would be a long and hard comeback.

After several days in the hospital, we finally had Eric home and I went back to attending my graduate classes. A week after Eric's surgery I was invited to breakfast with the dean, along with a handful of other students. It was during this small event that I found out that I had won the Jameson Preaching Award, given to one student every year chosen by the faculty. I was so shocked and deeply humbled, first, because I did not know the school had this type of award and second, because they chose me. Immediately following the breakfast, which detailed the upcoming public announcements of the awards, I called my bedridden and slightly drugged husband. He was so ecstatic for me. I then reached out to my family on our sibling text.

I was reading their congratulatory messages while waiting for my routine ultrasound appointment at my obstetrician's office. Within minutes of when the ultrasound started, I knew something was wrong. I could see my baby but the machine was not picking up a heartbeat. I had been through enough ultrasounds to know something was wrong. I looked at the radiology tech, who kept rolling the machine over my abdomen in search of what I knew wasn't there. She looked at me and said, "I am going to need to get someone to talk to you, okay?"

"Something is wrong, isn't it? I know it."

"Please let me get someone to talk to you, okay?" she said. I nodded.

I sat in the dark lit exam room and stared down at my belly. The tears began to fall amidst the nausea I had been fighting for months. Some brief time later, a wonderful Black midwife entered with the ultrasound tech, who was also a Black woman. They told me that my baby had no heartbeat. I sobbed; they stayed with me as I wept. The midwife waited until I asked, "What's next?" before she set up another appointment for me with the doctor. When the midwife left, she offered her condolences, leaving me and the woman tech in the room. When I got off the bed, she hugged me, held me, and whispered care to me. The presence of those two women gave me enough strength to make the follow-up appointment and walk to my car.

I called Eric first. This was the one of the very few times he was not able to be at my side throughout all of our children's prenatal visits. He wept with me. Then he raged. "Does the world have something against us right now?! Why is all this happening?" Also add in a few choice curse words sprinkled throughout.

Next, I sent a text on the very same family thread I was on just minutes before and The Sallehs took the news with heartbreak and dark humor: "Only you, "T", could have us jumping up in excitement and congratulations one minute and then in the throes of devastation the next. Please refrain from texting us for at least a day as we just try to manage one hour of your life." I do not know why but I just cackled at their responses. My family can make me laugh at all the wrong and oh-so-right times. There I sat in the car, talking to my cursing husband who raged with me, and reading texts from family who made me laugh through the tears. In that parking lot on that day, I found the wide expanse of emotions offered in communal grief-sharing.

Eric and I told our children and they cried with us. I

also described the steps that needed to be taken because my body wasn't letting go. The day of my procedure, my mother accompanied me and afterwards, I came home to my children's hugs and tears. After a slow walk upstairs, I went to my bed to bleed and heal. Somewhere in the middle of the night, I woke to change my pad and found all four children asleep around our bed. They had brought their blankets and pillows, found spaces on the floor to sleep. Together they formed something akin to a human nest, with me in the midst. Their sleeping forms were a stark reminder that there was still life in loss. They were holding me, surrounding me in not only *my* loss but *our* loss. I returned to bed, grateful that my children had chosen to swaddle me.

LOVE SHOWED UP AS A CHILD'S NEST AND SHOWERED ME IN THE LIVING. AS A RECIPIENT OF THIS ACT OF LOVE ABUNDANT, I COMMIT TO SHOWING A LOVE THAT SURROUNDS.

KINGDOM CALCULUS

THE SAME SEMESTER OF MY MISCARRIAGE and Eric's double knee surgery, I had four pretty demanding graduate courses. I missed several classes when Eric had surgery. I also missed a few more classes when I had my D and C procedure and I was woefully behind. All of these hard life happenings were at the end of the semester, when deadlines for final papers and exams were fast approaching. I spoke with all my professors and my preceptors (graduate teaching assistants). They all encouraged me to finish the semester and try not to take an Incomplete because then it would be hard to catch up and graduate on time. With their urging, along with their extended deadlines, I trudged ahead to try and finish during spring semester 2015.

As I delved into my extensive and lengthy papers on liberation theology and womanism, Xavier, then ten years old, complained for several days about his ear hurting. I gave him some ibuprofen which helped, but as soon as the medicine wore off, he complained again. It wasn't until he was out playing basketball with a group of friends that one of the mothers brought him home early because he had stopped playing, complaining of his ear. Xavier was in tears. I decided to take him to Urgent Care because this kid didn't stop playing basketball for nothing, so he must be suffering. The kind physician's assistant examined Xavier and said, "Ouch! You almost have a perforated eardrum. This must be so painful for you, buddy." Xavier looked at me and said, "I told you I was in pain, Mom." I immediately felt like poop. I had been so busy taking care of Eric, post-surgery and bedridden, and trying to attend classes and finish assignments, that I did not pay close enough attention to the pain of my child.

Years ago, I had made a promise to myself that I would not allow the academy and/or my professional life take precedence over my family when they truly needed me. So, there I sat, realizing that I was so busy trying to finish the semester that I had minimized Xavier's pain. I looked at Xay and began apologizing. My sweet son smiled and said, "It's okay, Mom. There's been a lot going on." I continued apologizing: "I still should have seen and heard you better, and for that I am sorry, son. I will do better." Xavier, along with his siblings, has this great capacity to forgive me and seemingly move on. I am indeed grateful for the grace they extend to me in my motherhood and personhood. (With that said, we also offer therapy and ways that they can healthily navigate being raised by flawed human beings.)

We came home from Urgent Care with a strict regimen of medicine every four hours to heal Xavier's eardrum. That night, I made sure to give Eric his series of meds on his time schedule and added Xavier's schedule to the mix. When the house was quiet and everyone was medicated, it seemed (except me), I got to work on my papers. By 1 a.m. it was time to wake Xavier and Eric for their medicines. In a daze I tried to read pill bottles and dosages. Xavier was hard to rouse, and he certainly didn't like being awakened to take another dose of two nasty meds. I went to put my feet in my house shoes and found that the dog had vomited in my slippers. She, too, was sick. I just broke. The puke in my house shoes was the last straw and I started yelling in the middle of the night, rousing the whole house. I screamed something to the effect of "Are you kidding me? Why can't the dog puke anywhere else?! Why, why, why???"

The house went eerily silent. I knew I had awakened the house but no one dared interrupt my middle-of-the-night lament. I eventually calmed down. Gave folks their medicine. Cleaned up puke and made a note to take Lucy to the vet. I got back to writing my papers in tears.

I made the extended deadlines and probably handed in some of the worst work of my academic career. I had finished. I felt defeated and partly embarrassed for what I turned in, but I had finished.

Days later, I got enough courage to check my grades, praying that I passed all four courses but preparing for impending failure. I looked and I had the highest GPA thus far (A, A, A-, A-). What in the world?! This was not possible.

I contacted my teachers and preceptors to confirm my grades and partly to ask "How?" Their answers all mimicked one another: "That's your grade. It may not be what you think you earned, but it is what you were given."

My Christian Theology professor, Dr. Willie Jennings, once taught us about "Kingdom Calculus." The math of the Divine — a higher math where God's grace makes up the difference. My grades during spring semester of 2015, while undergoing a miscarriage, a son with a perforated ear drum, a husband with two broken knees, and a vomiting dog, somehow showed that I had done A level work.

Kingdom Calculus, indeed.

LOVE SHOWED UP AS KINGDOM CALCULUS AND SHOWERED ME IN GRACE. AS A RECIPIENT OF THIS ACT OF LOVE ABUNDANT, I COMMIT TO SHOWING A LOVE THAT WORKS IN THE MATH OF THE DIVINE.

BAKED MACARONI

MY AUNT CAROL, WHO DIED OF COVID in February 2020, was the best cook. Her baked macaroni was one of my favorite recipes. Long after we moved away from New York, I called her every Thanksgiving for years to have her walk me through her recipe. Auntie Carol was one of those cooks that just cooked. There was no recipe outside of the one in her head. She had made this dish so many times that she just knew measurements by sight. Unfortunately, I did not have her sight, which made it hard for a fledgling foodie. I do know that every year for about eight years straight, I called her like clockwork to ask how I could make her dish. She stayed on the phone with me through the complicated parts. Other years, I called every one or two steps.

One year, I didn't look at the labels and used sweetened condensed milk instead of evaporated milk. The macaroni was sickening sweet. Another year, I added too much pepper and my family tried hard not to gag in front of me. After each failure, I would call Auntie and let her know how bad it went. She laughed with her hearty laugh. I couldn't help but smile that my mishaps made for her yearly entertainment.

A few years before she passed, she called me before Thanksgiving to ask if I was making baked macaroni. I said this was the year that I thought I could do it on my own. I could hear the smile in her voice when she assured me that I was more than capable. The next day, she called to follow up. I started cheering because I had finally made it without bothering her. Now, the dish wasn't nearly as good as hers, but it was edible without gagging and that was a win for me. Auntie Carol patiently told me that I never bothered her. It was good to hear from me and all my stories of the kitchen.

This year I made her dish. I wish I could have called her and told her that this was the closest I had come to her recipe, but it still wasn't it. It's a special kind of love that lets you nag your Auntie year after year, and she patiently shares again and again and again how to make your favorite dish. I miss her cooking. She used to tell me that I needed to just cook right beside her in the kitchen, and it would better coalesce. I never got that opportunity. Until we meet in that Heavenly kitchen, I will rely on the years of her wonderful guidance and infinite patience.

LOVE SHOWED UP AS AUNTIE CAROL'S <u>BAKED MACARONI</u> AND SHOWERED ME IN <u>PATIENCE</u>. AS A RECIPIENT OF THIS ACT OF LOVE ABUNDANT, I COMMIT TO SHOWING A LOVE THAT <u>IS MORE THAN HAPPY TO REVIEW AGAIN AND AGAIN.</u>

NOT A DOG PERSON

WHEN I MARRIED ERIC, he immediately told me that cats were not in our future together. He liked dogs. Not just any dogs: pit bulls. This distinct difference about the best kind of pet kept our home animal-free for more than a decade, despite the kids always asking for one.

On June 20, 2013, my husband lost his mother, Meriden Foster. She was a wonderful woman and I loved her. She always took my side when I told her about her son. She was a terrific grandmother and spoiled our children. She quilted them blankets, made them memory books, and always remembered all our birthdays. The cards and envelopes with her small and careful cursive came like clockwork. While Eric did not necessarily shed many tears in the immediate days leading up to Meriden's funeral and afterwards, he began to be distant and withdrawn. Solemn.

A few months after his mother's death, Eric asked me if he could adopt a dog. "No" was still my answer. In all honesty, I had a healthy and well-founded fear of dogs, having been bitten by one while serving a church mission in Brazil. Yet Eric kept talking to me about it. Of course, he had no problem having our children join his campaign. I finally agreed that we could merely LOOK at the dogs in the shelter. Just look. No promises. Also, one big condition: the dog needed to show that they would be good around our children. I thought that would be the hardest part because our four children were, as they say in the South, "wide open."

When we finally went to the local animal shelter, there were so many dogs. While I did try to steer us to the cat section, nobody was listening. I walked the long aisle perusing the dogs and found not a single one that I liked. Well, I was ready to go home, my job done here.

But Eric and our four kiddos walked the aisle a few times and then Eric asked about a brown and white mixed pitbull named Lucy. From her eyes, we didn't know if she had an issue with sight. She looked sad. She seemed to be the only dog not barking. The sign said that she might not be good with young children. Still, Eric was drawn to her, and our children heartily agreed. They ushered our family into a waiting room and then brought Lucy in. She immediately wagged her tail, rolled unto her back and showed her belly in complete trust of six new people. She showed a level of excitement and acceptance that completely belied her behavior in the kennel. Everyone fell in love with her — except me. I told Eric and the kids we would go home and think about it since it was such a big decision.

The next day while I was in class, I received a text from Eric. He showed me a picture of Lucy in our van on her way to her new home, our home. I was so livid. I text-yelled at Eric. He replied that he and the children just had to go back to get her. The nature of this forced adoption put me and

Lucy at odds for more than a year. I patted her head once or twice a day, took her to the vet, but otherwise ignored her. In response to my deliberate distance, Lucy drew near. She followed me around, sat on top of my feet when I was standing, and came to me when she needed to eat, walk, and be petted. I tried. I really did try to keep from liking Lucy, but Lucy refused to accept my semi-rejection and instead called for closeness.

I noticed she had a profound relationship with everyone, especially Eric. Lucy let Eric weep. At times, I would catch him holding and petting Lucy and her fur would catch his tears. For some good Godly reason, this dog offered space for Eric's grief. Lucy helped Eric grieve. I see now why Eric needed this dog. When Eric couldn't sleep at nights, she stayed up with him. She went on long walks to the rivers and lakes with him. And when Lucy got real sick at the end, right before we took her to the vet, she gingerly climbed on our bed and waited for Eric. He came home, saw her there (she was so sick then), and my husband wept again into her. She was saying her goodbye.

Lucy was just not Eric's companion but a friend to us all. She stayed by Micah's side when he had the flu. Twice. In one month. She slept with Xavier and when he withdrew from us in his early teenage years, Lucy seemed to be the only living entity that could draw him out. She grew with Ronin and taught him to care for her as they both got older. Lucy gave so many kisses to Zora that as a toddler, she often parked herself near the dog, just to get her full set of wet licks that often spiraled into a giggle fest.

I learned to love this dog, and you can't tell me she didn't love me. She drew me near even as I asked for distance. Before Lucy, I was not a dog person, but I became a Lucy person. And yes, she worked such a love for me that she made me a dog person.

My children have their own stories to tell. Lucy was the dog who let us grieve. She loved us when some of us were not as inclined to love her. I am grateful for Lucy's life. Lucy's passing in 2021 devastated us all. Indeed, some of my greatest humanity was found in the love of a dog.

LOVE SHOWED UP AS <u>A DOG'S LIFE</u> AND SHOWERED ME IN <u>COMPANIONSHIP</u>. AS A RECIPIENT OF THIS ACT OF LOVE ABUNDANT, I COMMIT TO SHOWING A LOVE THAT <u>VALUES THE RELATIONSHIPS OFFERED BY GOD'S CREATURES.</u>

GINNY'S FINAL WORDS

AT 18, I MET GINNY during our freshman year at Utah State University. We were roommates and began a friendship that would span a lifetime. Most days she entered our dorm room, sat on my bed, and said, "Please tell me about your day." For some reason, Ginny treated my accounts of my daily happenings like circle time in an elementary classroom. She laughed out loud often, cried sometimes, but always patiently waited until the end to ask her questions. Always questions that let you know she was deeply listening; her questions were part of her listening. She liked wrapping herself in the stories of others. It's what made her a great English major.

At 21, we both decided to serve Latter-day Saint missions and ended up at the Missionary Training Center during the same two-month period. It was so comforting so see her occasionally throughout those weeks while we both struggled to learn our respective languages. She was learning Cantonese to serve in Hong Kong, and I was learning Portuguese for Brazil. Whenever we caught each other between classes, we would nearly run to the other and squeeze.

We reunited a year and a half later after our missions,

picking up where we left off, just full of stories. Now at two different Utah colleges, Ginny and I arranged to take religion classes together in the community so we could see one another. Before I knew it, Ginny found someone to love who loved her. She asked me to be in her wedding party and I accepted.

I can't tell you why or how I forgot her wedding day but I did. May 16, 1999. I didn't show up to the wedding. She called me on her wedding day to tell me how angry she was that I missed her day.

In true Ginny fashion, she didn't raise her voice, but her deep disappointment was almost a whisper that I heard loud and clear. My heart sank. No profuse set of apologies was going to make up for my absence. I knew that and I still apologized. I made it to the reception in time to staff the sign-in book, per one of my duties. I caught her in a hug before she and husband left and whispered another apology. She replied, "It will take me some time to forgive you for this. I just don't know how you could have missed this day with me."

I married Eric a few years later. At the time, Ginny was living out of the country and could not attend my wedding. For the next few years, we reached out to one another sporadically as we both tried to regain our friendship. It was harder now that we were geographically separated and completely submerged in the early days of marriage and motherhood. We both ended up with four children, three boys and a girl.

As our kiddos got older, things seemed less heartbroken between us and we started reaching out more readily. One day I woke with Ginny on my heart and I felt the strong urge to reach out to her. I picked up my phone and called my friend. After our salutations, I told her that out of nowhere I had this strong feeling to call her. My friend then took a deep breath and said, "I have been trying and trying to find a way to call you and tell you something, but I just haven't found the words to tell you."

"Tell me what, Ginny?" I asked, scared.

"I have stage four colon cancer, and it's bad. But I am still hopeful."

I heard the resolve in my friend's voice, and I fully believed her. Surely she could beat it long enough to raise her children, who ranged from teenagers to a toddler. As my tears quietly formed and fell, we carried on a long conversation about her faith and fight. When she tired of cancer talk, she asked me to fill our time with my stories. Not since our college roommate days had she asked me to just tell her the stories of my days. So, when my friend of more than twenty-five years asked me to take her into my life, just like old times, I gladly obliged. Just like that, we transported ourselves to a college dorm in 1993. Yet this time, I spoke of my children, my husband, and my latest efforts to find myself, again. Ginny laughed and listened. And when we ended our talk, she thanked me for calling.

"I feel better now that you know, Fatimah."

Ginny lived more than a year after her diagnosis. She passed away on May 24, 2018 at 43. Not before I flew across the country from North Carolina to Utah to visit her at her home. Not before we shared waffles at a local diner. Not before she and I curled up on her sofa and chatted for hours. Not before we hugged each other tight every chance we got. Not before we captured and held on tight to our friendship of so many years.

In her final days, I called her as she was "actively dying" at home with her husband and children. Her husband, Nate, set up a video call and in our brief connection, we both realized we were wearing bright yellow nail polish "to welcome summer," Ginny said. Nate snapped a picture of us both showing off our nail polish to one another with big grins on our faces.

Then Ginny told me she was tired and that she would talk to me later. We expressed our love for one another.

There would be no more conversations with Ginny. This was her last one with me.

When Nate called to tell me of my friend's passing, he told me that Ginny wanted me to give her eulogy and tell her story. I wept when he asked. Of course, I would share my final story-sharing time at Ginny's memorial service.

For someone who specialized in listening, I hope she heard me that day when I told all those in attendance about the wonder and marvel that was Ginny. I especially spoke to her four children, hoping they might remember the words of an old friend about the legacy of listening and kindness that was embodied in their mother.

LOVE SHOWED UP AS A <u>FRIEND'S FORGIVENESS</u> AND SHOWERED ME IN <u>DEEP LISTENING</u>. AS A RECIPIENT OF THIS ACT OF LOVE ABUNDANT, I COMMIT TO SHOWING A LOVE THAT <u>LISTENS.</u>

UNICORN STYLZ

WHEN THE PANDEMIC HIT IN 2020 and our four children were sent home, Zora (age eight) was finishing second grade. She had a lot of time on her hands, and her hands found brushes and makeup. In my then-45 years of life, I had never really worn makeup. While my three sisters are practically makeup magicians, I, for some reason, never really felt the need to experiment and learn how to apply it. Yet God gave me a daughter, and she loves doing hair and makeup.

With Zora's newfound exorbitant time at home, she decided to open her own salon, Unicorn Stylz. I was her only client. Zora's experiments on my looks are nothing new. I remember specifically early one morning when she was three years old and I was still laying in my bed. Zora was already up, bringing water to my face to "help me clean my face." After my fourth or fifth dousing of water, I asked where she was getting all this water. This is probably a question I should have asked sooner. "The toilet," she promptly and proudly replied.

This was just the beginning of our understanding — I was susceptible to her makeover machinations and in return, she was busy and happy. Fast forward five years, and I readily agreed to be Zora's sole client at Unicorn Stylz (her spelling, not mine). Throughout the two years of quarantine, I have donned many faces from the Joker to a kitty cat. My hair has been pulled, brushed, styled, and sprayed. At times, because this activity kept Zora so happy, I allowed her to style my hair while I was on Zoom calls for work. My colleagues were overly understanding, and I think, from their muted giggles, slightly entertained. Zora's makeovers remain both a spectacle and a highlight to my time in quarantine with a lil' person. Zora always snapped a picture after completing her work on me. Subsequently, I collected a bevy of pictures on my phone showcasing her work.

LOVE SHOWED UP AS A MAKEOVER AND SHOWERED ME IN EYE SHADOWS, BLUSH, LIPSTICK AND CONCEALER. AS A RECIPIENT OF THIS ACT OF LOVE ABUNDANT, I COMMIT TO SHOWING A LOVE THAT IS OPEN TO LOOKING SILLY AND BEING THRILLED ABOUT IT.

DEFIANT FRIENDSHIP

SHORTLY AFTER GIVING BIRTH to Zora Grace in 2012 and receiving my PhD in mass communication three months later, I hit one of the hardest periods of my life. Even with my doctorate degree, it seemed that I could not land a job anywhere. For more than a year I filled out copious applications to colleges all over the nation for professor positions. Not only did I not get a job I so desperately needed, I did not even make it to a single interview. My white colleagues had all been hired at various institutions. Some of them had not even finished their dissertations, but were seemingly more hirable than me.[1] My progress (or lack thereof) in acquiring gainful employment was so dismal that Dr. Jane Brown, my mentor and dissertation chair, called me in to check on me. In our meeting she asked about where I had applied, and she agreed that I had cast a wide net. Then she offered to take a look at my application materials. Meticulously, just as she did everything, she reviewed my

---

1. See, for example, Dina Gerdeman, "Minorities Who 'Whiten' Job Resumes Get More Interviews," *Harvard Business School*, May 17, 2017. According to the National Science Foundation's Survey of Earned Doctorates, 4.4% of doctoral degrees were earned by Black women in 2012. See nsf.gov/statistics/srvydoctorates/.

C.V., writing sample, and list of recommenders. She found nothing askew. Finishing her review, Jane sighed. "We (the faculty within the college) just do not know why you are not getting any chances to even interview…it's weird. Hang in there, Fatimah, and let me know if I can do anything."

Weird was an understatement. I guess I should have also let her know that I did offer a prayer months ago that if I was not meant for a job, that God would keep me from the interview process. The interview rigamarole for college faculty tended to be both an extensive and rigorous process. In truth, I did not want to fly out to a school and go through the intense two or three day interview process if it was not where I was meant to be. Time and energy were limited resources for mamas. And this mother was already exhausted, with a baby and three other young children. I usually am careful about what I pray for, and while I still do not regret this prayer, I did not realize how hard it would be on my self-esteem to be overlooked by so many, so often. Many did not even bother to tell me that I did not get the position; I just found out that they had hired someone else.

After nearly a year of no one taking an interest in me, I was angry. I wondered why I had stepped into so much debt and spent so much time on three letters behind my name that could not get me a single job interview. I was so enraged one day that I took a look at my fancy diploma, hanging up in its fancy frame and I yanked it off the wall. The degree mocked me. It had promised me something. It was the promise that if I finished this hard thing, I could be a professor and I could teach. That was a lie. To this day, the frame on my diploma has a chip in it, where it hit a piece of furniture on its way down to the floor. I refused to rehang it until it offered me something more. Indeed, that diploma stayed unhung for several years.

No university wanted me as a teacher.

At this same time, I was heavily involved in my Latter-day Saint church community. In my home ward (congregation) I met two wonderful women, RaeAnn and Amy. Along with my sister Najah, we developed a friendship that called for regular get-togethers over breakfast, usually Amy's German pancakes with all the fixings, while our children (thirteen in total) ran amok around us. In this community-created cocoon, the four of us shared our lives, seeing each other through motherhood, wifedom, divorce, dating and single life, depression, schooling, graduations, and everything else life threw our way. At times life got pretty grueling for one or more of us, and our meetings would be adjusted to accommodate whoever needed our cocooned care.

During this time of unemployment, this friendship stemming from church sustained me. It continued to sustain me even when I left the church.

At this time, I was called to be a Sunday School teacher in my LDS ward. A group of women approached me after a lesson one day and asked if I would be willing to start a women's scripture study group. The plan they offered was to rotate between our homes and allow our children to come alongside, while I taught in a more casual environment that allowed for questions and conversation. I was thrilled at this invitation and more than happy to do something like this. While we women set to planning our first meeting, two members of the bishopric (male lay leaders of an LDS ward) asked to stop by my home to talk with me. As the two men sat on my sofa, they told me that they had heard of a women's group assembling outside of the church, where I would be teaching. Then they proceeded to ask me to refrain from holding these types of meetings especially since there would be no priesthood holder present to preside over the meetings.

To this day, I don't know why I agreed. Yes, I do. I agreed because they were my priesthood leaders. The leaders I had sustained and trusted. So, I said yes to their no. And oof, did this hurt.

Within a few months of this leadership-imposed sanction, some LDS college students asked me to offer a talk on a topic of my choice with one caveat: that I leave time for their questions and ensuing discussion. This request was a little outside the normal LDS culture (usually a leader would do the inviting) but again, I was thrilled to engage them. I had previously taught a college-level religion class that was so full that students lined the hallway outside the classroom. But for some unknown reason, I was never invited back to teach again.

I was so thrilled these college students had asked for me specifically to speak with them. The heavens knew that

I could not seem to get a job teaching at a college, so it was even sweeter that they sought me out and honored me with their invitation. The day before I was to give my talk, the director of the Institute (LDS college students program) called me to cancel. He relayed to me that the Church's priesthood leadership had come to the decision that it would not be best for me to engage with the young adults in the program, because they, the leadership, were not certain as to my testimony and what I would exactly share with the students. Ultimately, I might be a poor influence.

I sat on the phone in shock and then the questions came flooding through. What in my steady church attendance, tithe-paying, call-magnifying work within the ward had made priesthood leadership concerned about my testimony? What in the world could make me a poor influence? Once the shock wore off, I was extremely hurt and then I got really pissed off. Consequently, I requested a meeting with our highest local church leadership (called the stake presidency) in response to their decision. After two such meetings a few things were made clear to me: one, I was perceived as having an "attitude problem and needed to work on my humility" and two, my political leanings in support of Barack Obama (who was running for presidential re-election at that time) were also a cause of worry.

My church did not want me as a teacher.

It wasn't until Eric gave Zora her baby blessing that I realized what I had been fighting for so long was something The Church of Jesus Christ of Latter-day Saints wouldn't ever give me — the ability to live fully into my own sense of calling. In Eric's blessing of our daughter, which only he and other men (priesthood holders) could offer, he blessed Zora that she would be able to live into her full potential. When he said those words, I knew deep down that my daughter would never be able to live fully in the LDS church, not as a woman, and definitely not as a woman of color. While I did not have enough willpower at that time to consider seriously leaving the church, I could not, in good conscience, subject my daughter to the same confines, especially if I had a choice about it.

I love teaching; it is a passion of mine, and part of my call in this world. Yet my efforts to just teach, no matter how hard I tried, I could not seem to escape both academic and religious institutions that did not want me teaching. I suppose if one or the other would have allowed me to live out some part of this desire, I would have been over-the-moon thrilled, but to have every teaching door I knocked on be closed, if not slammed in my face, was debilitating.

In one of my long conversations with my Mom, I was, once again, bemoaning my state — trying to find a way out. My Mom then had an idea, out of the blue: she asked me to call Dr. Josef Sorett, the son of her lifelong best friend. Jossef just happened to also be my long-standing friend too. I guess when your mothers have been best friends all your lives, you are likely to develop a friendship as well. I thought my Mom's suggestion was odd but what the heck?

I was all out of ideas and options of what to do with my unemployed, practically religiously disenfranchised life.

In my conversation with Josef, with my Mom listening all the while, I laid out my current and somewhat embarrassing life situation. Josef listened carefully and then said five words strewn together in both horror and holy direction: "You should get a MDiv."

"What?!" I replied, "What is that?"

"It's a Master of Divinity," he answered.

"I just finished a hundred years of school; I have taken my LAST graduate school class AND I am hundreds of thousands of dollars in student debt. I already have a masters and a PhD! I have no desire to go back to school. None. Zip. Zero. What I need is gainful employment, not more school!"

Josef laughed and said, "Duke Divinity School is right there; you should apply. Divinity school is the perfect place to work out all the questions you have about church and God. Just think about it."

And think about it I did. I had no other options. No other choices. So, I begrudgingly filled out an application to pursue a Master of Divinity at Duke. My personal letter was chock-full of church hurt, frustration, and resignation. They accepted me. I joke that it was one of the only acceptances to school that I might have mourned. Certainly, God did not intend for me to attend three more years of school. But God did. If there is one thing I learned about my own journey, it is that I do not always know what will make me happy. I think I know what will fulfill me, but I have slowly come to the sneaking suspicion that I have no idea. My imagination is too finite, in many ways too preconstructed and heavily prefabricated.

During my first year of seminary, I slowly backed away from the LDS faith. I stopped going to Sunday service every week. I started looking for other churches that could possibly accompany me as I found God anew.

Throughout this whole time, I stayed in faithful friendship and conversation with RaeAnn and Amy, still devout Latter-day Saints. They accompanied me as I tried to make myself fit into the LDS Church's confining constraints. They shared my frustration when I was told repeatedly that I could not teach, and stood with me when my testimony was questioned and disparaged. They raged and cried along with me. They hugged me and held on tight as I fought to stay in a church that ultimately, did not want me. When I started my slow and heartbreaking withdrawal from the LDS faith, everything about the prevailing doctrine said "I was lost" and had "fallen away." I was someone to be partly pitied, worried about, and most certainly needed prayer for my return. With my church attendance dwindling to eventually, nonexistent, I was seen and categorized as an "inactive member." Yet my friends remained that much more active in supporting and affirming the uncertain faith journey that was ahead of me. When I preached, they traveled far to attend the services. When I shared what I was learning in school, they got excited with me.

I cannot thank these two women enough for their radical friendship. While the LDS religion expected them to see and treat me differently, they did not. In fact, I felt the expansion and deepening of their love, all the while letting me know I was on the right track. Though my track did not look like their own, nor like my previous religious life, I was still on the right path. Their friendship and love helped carry me through when I thought I not only lost my church, but all those who I loved within it. But not them. Their love was going with me, wherever I traveled.

LOVE SHOWED UP AS <u>RADICAL FRIENDSHIP</u> AND SHOWERED ME IN <u>AFFIRMATION</u>. AS A RECIPIENT OF THIS ACT OF LOVE ABUNDANT, I COMMIT TO SHOWING A LOVE THAT <u>DEFIES RELIGIOUS UNDERSTANDING.</u>

FURTHER + MORE:

My dissertation research showed that Black women journalists heavily involved in the civil rights movement became far more radical and daring in their work after they had children. As if to say that while life was hard for them as individuals, they could take it, but what they could not take was that life would be this racist and sexist for their own children. For two of the three Black journalists I studied, motherhood propelled them to become more active in the justice movement. I found this was certainly the case for me as well. What I was unwilling to do for myself, I was brave enough to do for my daughter.

UNCLE GEORGE

IN 2018, I COULD NOT FIND MY FATHER. Last I heard from him, he was in a homeless shelter in Manhattan. During the years my father was homeless, he still found a way to contact me intermittently enough that I knew he was alive and as safe as he could be, considering his situation. But it had been months since I heard from him and I began to be worried.

I reached out to the homeless shelter where I thought he stayed, and they said he had left on his own accord. I contacted the barbershop where he spent some time, and they too were alarmed because they had not seen him in a long while. Then I called the *dojo*, where I knew he practiced his Aikido martial arts, but they had not seen him there either. I even called the NYPD and tried to place a missing person's report, but it is hard to do that for an unhoused Black senior person. I often say that my father is one of the only people I know who can live off the grid in one of the biggest cities in the country.

Scared and worried, I called the only person I knew who would take the time and had the skills to look for my father: my Uncle George.

Uncle George is my Nana's brother and the youngest of

the five. With four older sisters and as the only son, Uncle George had the best stories about his coming-of-age antics. One Thanksgiving, Nana and Uncle George got to telling stories. Throughout George's stories, Nana shook her head. "You always did like to run the streets," she kept saying, as if this was the answer for all the hilarity and mess that George got himself into.

My Uncle George played the numbers[1] as religiously as my four aunties went to Sunday service and Bible studies. He smoked, danced, and knew the streets of Manhattan and Brooklyn better than any GPS. Not only did he know how to navigate the streets, but he also knew folks and folks' families who lived on those streets.

When my father was released from prison,[2] Uncle George felt it was important that he learn to defend himself. Since he was now a convicted felon, my father couldn't carry a weapon. So Uncle George introduced my father to Sensei Elmo, who owned and taught at a judo and jiujitsu *dojo*. How my uncle knew a jiujitsu teacher when he had never taken a class, I have no idea. This one introduction would launch my father's long and beautiful life as a martial artist. In this matchup, Uncle George introduced my father to one

---

1. Playing the numbers is a form of lottery that arose in the Harlem Renaissance.
2. At 19, my father went to prison. He confessed to a crime he did not commit to save another young man from going to prison. My father served a year and a half at Rikers Island prison. His friend, Felipe Luciano, wrote in his biography *Flesh and Spirit: Confessions of a Young Lord*, about my father's confession despite his innocence.

of the greatest loves of my dad's life. My father's love with martial arts would outlast most of his human relationships.

Even during my father's self-imposed estrangement from his family, Uncle George would routinely find my Dad or run into him on the streets. Inevitably, Uncle would call me to let me know my father was okay. I think George understood how important it was to me that I knew my father was okay even though he was unwilling to be in relationship with me or any of us. More than anyone, Uncle George knew my seemingly irrational desire to see about my father, a man who didn't always want to see about me. George also regularly sought out his own father, my great grandfather, who nearly abandoned them.

When I called Uncle George, he knew what I was asking before I could ask. He offered before the words could form in my mouth. That's one of the reasons I just loved my uncle. Over the next few weeks, Uncle George scoured the streets of New York to find my father. He visited my father's old haunts and a few of his lifelong friends and still found nothing. Uncle George even went to hospitals and morgues, keeping me updated all the while.

After a few weeks, Uncle George found out that my father was at a Brooklyn homeless shelter. But he didn't find him at the shelter. No, he found him at a senior citizen center that provided breakfast and lunch. Upon finding him, Uncle George had my father leave me a voice message. I cried hearing my father's voice, knowing he was alright.

Only Uncle George.

Only Uncle George could spend weeks finding my father among eight million people in one of the biggest cities in the nation, all at the behest of his grandniece.

When Uncle George passed away in January 2020, his daughter, my cousin Leslie, asked me to speak at his funeral. The first thing I did was play a voicemail he had left me years ago. It was simple. In his deep, gravelly voice, all he said was, "Hey, Timah, this is your Uncle George. Do me a favor and call your grandmother; she wants to hear from you. Take care." I wanted to let everyone know that I, too, was found by my Great (The Great) Uncle George. He found people for people.

LOVE SHOWED UP AS MY GREAT UNCLE GEORGE AND SHOWERED ME IN IRRATIONAL UNDERSTANDING. AS A RECIPIENT OF THIS ACT OF LOVE ABUNDANT, I COMMIT TO SHOWING A LOVE THAT FINDS PEOPLE FOR PEOPLE.

FURTHER + MORE:

Uncle George was the only person who knew where my father could be found. It escaped me that I should have asked Uncle for a physical address. So, when George passed, I lost the only person who knew how to locate Dad.

Within a month of Uncle's funeral, I got a call from

Ms. Lois who worked at a senior center in Brooklyn. She wanted to let me know that she saw my father daily. She asked my Dad for any information on his family and got my phone number. Ms. Lois told me that she would keep a good watch on my father and keep me posted. Since Ms. Lois's call, a string of social workers, homeless shelter personnel, and administrators have all reached out to me to let me know that they would be happy to serve as a connector for me and my father. Since that day, for more than two and a half years, I have not lost contact with my father. Now I know where he is, because we helped him get an apartment and I had a phone installed.

 Thank you, Uncle George, for loving me in this life and into the hereafter. Sometimes love, especially love like his, just keeps on going, long after he has physically left us.

PASTORAL REASSURANCE

IN THE SUMMER OF 2021, after much prayer and pondering, I called Pastor Arlee Arkofa to tell him that I was withdrawing my name as a minister in our church. I stated my reasons, chief among them being that my theology was expanding, deepening in ways that stretched my own understanding of God and Christianity. And I did not want to bear the name of the church if my erupting theology was not going to represent or be at odds with their theology.

In the softest and nicest way I've ever heard, Pastor said, "No."

He continued, "I do not have to agree or even fully understand your theology to affirm you. I know you know God. You go and do what God calls you to do and we, as a church, are here. We affirm you and we support you."

*cue my weeping

"Are you sure?" I asked. (Because in truth I was even unsure of this radical faith journey of mine.)

"I am not afraid of your courage," he said. Then repeated himself—

"I am not afraid of your courage."

LOVE SHOWED UP AS <u>SUPPORT</u> AND SHOWERED ME IN <u>AFFIRMATION</u>. AS A RECIPIENT OF THIS ACT OF LOVE ABUNDANT, I COMMIT TO SHOWING A LOVE THAT <u>IS NOT AFRAID OF ANOTHER'S COURAGE.</u>

PASTOR PEOPLE

WHEN I BEGAN MY SLOW WITHDRAWAL from the LDS religion, I felt the immediate and sizeable void that the absence of the church left in my life. For more than twenty years I had belonged to a wonderful community of Saints, and so much of my personal and social life orbited around this religious community. I knew I needed some place to go, some place to worship on Sundays in a large attempt to fill the chasm. To date, my decision to find God elsewhere, outside of the LDS faith, was one of the scariest times in my life. For so many years, the church had provided me with a guiding anchor, a loving and supportive community, and a place for my family. Now that was gone.

For almost two years, I let myself religiously wander. As I ventured into the vast unknown of the extensive and myriad Christian churches, I had the keen blessing of being loved and guided by some pretty awesome pastor people. One thing divinity school offered me, among many, was the chance to meet a cadre of clergy and faithful members from different religious denominations. As it turns out, seminary is the perfect place for religious uncertainty and holy exploration. Prior to Duke Divinity, I knew of only one Reverend Doctor and that was Rev. Dr. Martin Luther

King Jr.; turns out there's quite a few of them running around. Much like every memory shared in this book, the following accounts only begin to touch on the magic of these encounters. Here are some of the many pastors whose ministry and love not only changed me but changed the way I know to pastor.

AN UNRULY SPIRITUAL JOURNEY

PASTORAL PEOPLE

THE REV. LIZ DOWLING-SENDOR ("LIZ") led my first required course in divinity school, "Spiritual Formation." I detested the fact that it was mandatory to take a spiritual formation class. In my ignorant estimation, all we did, all year long, once a week, was check in with one another, share our faith journeys, and learn about different spiritual disciples and practices. I tell you what — I did not want to share nothing with nobody. What was there to share? I was lost. I had no idea where I was going or even why God had landed me back in school at 38. I did not want to share and I certainly did not want to hear other people's stories that were certain to be filled with their certainty. It is safe to say that I was quite resistant to this class. The fact that I was required to take it all year made it all the more frustrating. My tumultuous faith journey was not fodder for academic course work; there were places for that, and a Duke classroom wasn't one.

That frustration died when it met the force of gentleness that is Rev. Liz. The spirit she brought to the classroom each week was filled with care, patience, and so much grace. She was a thoroughly intentional listener with no judgments, steaming with observable curiosity. Through her presence,

I learned about listening and, more importantly still, the healing touch of genuine curiosity. The way she honed our space together opened the pathway for us to share ourselves. And no, my classmates' stories were not filled with certainty, but with an unruly and complicated faith that was anything but strait and narrow. In the blessing of hearing Rev. Liz speak of her own religious and spiritual sojourn, I found the words and the affirmation in my own. She shared her own story with careful confidence, with all its twists and turns in disparate churches and religions. She named God at all her crossroads and seismic spiritual changes.

In the presence of The Rev. Liz Dowling-Sendor I learned to not only accept my own winding faith journey but embrace it. She showed me a God that was with me; a God that had never left me despite my perceived religious transience. Rev. Liz fostered my excitement to see what was next, while also allowing me to work through my feelings of divine betrayal and replace it with a deep gratitude for my religious experience. She pastored me through my grief, led me to acceptance, and eventually taught me to embrace this wild and unruly journey with an untamed God. It took a school year, once a week, under the tutelage of a good pastor, to do that painstaking work.

LOVE SHOWED UP AS <u>AN AFFIRMING FORCE</u> AND SHOWERED ME IN <u>SACRED STORY SHARING</u>. AS A RECIPIENT OF THIS ACT OF LOVE ABUNDANT, I COMMIT TO SHOWING A LOVE THAT <u>BOTH SHARES AND HOLDS ANOTHER'S STORY WITH REVERENCE.</u>

RADICAL WELCOME
PASTORAL PEOPLE

DUKE'S MASTER OF DIVINITY PROGRAM requires two Field Education experiences, akin to internships. After my first year of classes, I was assigned to serve at a local UMC (United Methodist Church) for the summer. The Field Education office placed me at a nearby church, being considerate of my family demands and responsibilities. (Some students' assignments took them across the nation and even out of the country for the summer. So I was grateful to be placed somewhere so close to home.) The pastor of the church where I was to serve reached out to me and we set up a meeting time. Somewhere in between the time we talked and our scheduled meeting, he decided he did not want me serving at his church. He called to tell me I wouldn't be a "good fit for their congregation," and that his church (a predominantly white congregation in 2014) had decided to forego a Duke intern for the summer.

    I was so hurt. This man just rejected me before he had even met me. We had not even had a full conversation, outside of scheduling a time to meet. Yet he and his church decided I was not what they wanted. I was still so tender and broken from my string of rejections in the LDS church that this last one from the UMC felt like another stinging slap at my latest attempt to live out my call.

I went back to my Field Ed. Office and spoke with the leadership there. My assigned pastor had left them a scathing message about placing someone like me with people like them. Matt Floding, then Director for Field Education, said he did not even bother to fully listen to the message. I admit I cried in Matt's office. I was so sick of the Church and its rejection of me. I was sick of male religious leadership who exercised a racist and sexist power over me. I told Matt that they should not send me to any church, certainly not one with male leadership, because I was done answering to patriarchy and begging for a small place at their tables. I was done asking men in the church, any church, to affirm me and accept what I had to offer as I tried to serve.

Rev. Matt listened and gently reminded me that in order to complete my degree, I needed to complete two Field Education credits. And after some deliberation, they decided to send me to someone who was safer and had a long-standing and beautiful relationship with the program: Rev. Rich Greenway at Union Grove Church in Hillsborough, North Carolina.

Rich, as he asked to be called, met me over lunch and I was immediately suspicious of him — a white, Southern clergyman with an easy disposition. Yup, not to be trusted. When we started our conversation, I said little to nothing. He engaged me by first apologizing for my experience with the previously assigned UMC pastor. He then told me that he would be thrilled and honored to work with me.

"I am excited to have you with us this summer, Fatimah. Welcome."

Day after day, all summer long, Rich welcomed me along with two other Duke Divinity interns. (Both would end up being good friends of mine.) This had to be the longest and deepest welcome I had ever encountered from a congregational leader.

He welcomed my ideas, even asking for them regularly throughout our meetings.

He welcomed my preaching, even as I preached a Black liberation womanist theology to a white Southern congregation.

He welcomed our children. Throughout my search for a new church home, my children had met no shortage of pastors from different congregations. Pastor Rich Greenway remains a beloved one to them.

Rich welcomed me when it felt like no one else would. In the cracks of the rejection and the unwelcome, Rich offered a radical welcome.

Rich not only preached welcome, but he also lived into it fully and wholly.

When he led communion, he made sure to remind folk that "All are welcome at the table."

At the end of worship service, Rich routinely invited all the visitors to make this their church home if they felt this was the place for them. "And if this is not a place where you feel you can make a home, please come see me. I would be happy to talk with you and see if any of the other churches in the area may be a good fit for you." I mean, who says that? Pastor Rich Greenway says that, and he means it.

As we neared the end of our time together, I asked if he thought I should try to go through the UMC ordination process. Rich was quiet and then said, "You are meant for ordination, and I would love to have you in our midst, but I do not know if the UMC could hold you well." Rich knew me well enough that he could simultaneously affirm me while also steering me away from spaces that wouldn't offer me the fullest extent of welcome.

Pastor Rich Greenway walks in welcome and just when I needed him most, he showed me how it's done.

LOVE SHOWED UP AS <u>A DESPERATELY NEEDED WELCOME</u> AND SHOWERED ME IN A <u>PASTORAL EMBRACE</u>. AS A RECIPIENT OF THIS ACT OF LOVE ABUNDANT, I COMMIT TO SHOWING A LOVE THAT <u>KNOWS THE VALUE OF A GOOD AND WARM WELCOME.</u>

FURTHER + MORE:

While I was in divinity school, I was looking for a church for my family to attend. Rev. Dr. William Turner, who taught my Preaching into Social Crisis class, had been the pastor of Mt. Level Missionary Baptist Church for decades, and was one of the first people I approached in my search for a church to attend. Surprisingly, he asked me a few questions: Did I have children and what were their ages? What did I look for in a worship service? Where did I live and was I willing to travel? After a string of questions, Dr. Turner took a minute to take in my answers, then recommended two different churches of two different denominations. He did not, oddly enough, put forth his church. I asked him why. "Oh! You are most certainly welcomed to come to my church. I hope you know that. I was thinking about you and your family's needs and desires for a church home, and those are the churches that immediately came to mind. I know the pastors of these churches, so if you would like me to introduce you, I would be happy to do that." I had never witnessed a pastor triage my church needs, and then, on top of that, suggest local churches. In the years to follow, I preached at Dr. Turner's church and sat in the pews on special occasions. Rev. Dr. William Turner, along with Rev. Rich Greenway, taught me the importance of knowing fellow pastors.

RELIGIOUS REFUGEE

PASTORAL PEOPLE

MY SECOND AND LAST FIELD EDUCATION was with Rev. Dr. Byron Benton ("Byron"), of Berean Baptist Church in Raleigh. Two of my Divinity school friends recommended I visit the church. My classmates were aware of my search for a church home and regularly suggested certain churches, which they either belonged to or had heard good things. It's actually quite lovely, now looking back, that my community of seminarians took such an active part in helping me find a church home. As a religious refugee, still in deep need of a church, I made sure to follow up on almost every recommendation. I can honestly say that in more than a year of searching, I found good and God at every service. As heartbreaking as it was to be longing for a community, I settled into the nomadic ways of sitting in new places, with varying theologies and church cultures. I have taken communion that was both water and wine, both wafer and homemade bread. I have both stood in line with fellow parishioners to await the holy serving, and I have sat in pews as I was served. During this time, I partly learned to settle into the unsettling nature of wandering. I say partly because I am still working on that settling.

I visited Berean Baptist Church on a rare occasion without my children in tow. I fully intended to slip in and out of this church unnoticed. So I came a little late, sat in the back, and hustled out of there as soon as the benediction's "Amen." During the worship service, I was handed a welcome card, and I absently filled it out. I did not hand it back but stuck it into the pages of my Bible. In the parking lot, a few feet from my getaway, one of the parishioners approached. Marco Trevino introduced himself and asked me about the service. He also noticed the card poking out of my scriptures. In the politest way possible, he asked if that was the visitors' card and if he could see it. I handed it over, knowing full well I put a non-working number on the card. It wasn't a lie, necessarily; it was just our landline that no one answered and had no phones actively connected to it. Marco looked at the card and said, "Is all this information correct and can we reach you at this phone number?"

I was caught. "Um, no. You can't really reach me at that number. Let me put the number of my cell phone."

He smiled and waited as I crossed out our landline and replaced it with my cell phone number. He then bid me goodbye with the hopes to see me again. Not more than two years later, Marco and I would be ordained together, side by side, as ministers of that church. I can't thank him enough for meeting me in the parking lot and asking me the one question that would inevitably bring me into the Berean fold. I found out later that he had taken my visitor's card straight to Pastor Byron and asked him to reach out to me personally.

I was a bit floored when Pastor Byron called my "real" number a few days later. He genuinely inquired about me and our family. In this initial conversation, I wanted Byron to know that my husband was not an avid church goer; he preferred the outdoors, mountains, rivers, and lakes to be with God.

"That's more than okay. We all have our ways to commune with God, no way better than another." There. Right there and those precise words, took me aback. I had never heard support of the notion that God could be found outside of the places dictated by man. This conversation had me back in Berean's pews, this time with my children. Eric attended occasionally to appease my incessant invitations, and eventually Berean won out more Sundays than the rivers and lakes. I eventually asked Byron if I could do my remaining field education experience with him, and he welcomed me. He would eventually see me through all the steps to my ordination.

In our weekly meetings, we discussed church polity, congregational needs, wrestled with scriptures and doctrine, and laughed. In one of my initial meetings, I honestly told Byron that I resented him and the fact that I had to go through yet another male gatekeeper to obtain ordination. (I was often grateful that Byron was getting his PhD in family and marriage therapy while he was working with me. This was one of the times.) He took a pregnant pause at my jab, looked at me with kindness and said, "How about I just journey alongside you and we work this out together? And I, too, am sorry for all the men that have hurt you in your desire to live out your call." He then asked for an ongoing dialogue that would serve as checks and balances for both of us as we moved in ministry, together.

A year and a half later, I was ordained the first woman minister at Berean Baptist Church in Raleigh. It was a long ordeal and not without its valleys. Yet when it was finished, Byron came to me and said, "You were ordained long before this. It takes us men a long time to catch up to God and we are often late."

Byron taught me about church hurt and intentionally worked alongside me so that I could simultaneously heal while pursing my call. I can't thank Rev. Dr. Byron Benton enough for walking alongside me when I was so wounded and tender. His pastoral work within me was filled with a deep carefulness and a mutual intentionality. He made me an active partner and empowered me to speak my truth to power.

LOVE SHOWED UP AS <u>A SOFT PLACE TO LAND</u> AND SHOWERED ME IN A <u>PASTORAL ACCOMPANIMENT</u>. AS A RECIPIENT OF THIS ACT OF LOVE ABUNDANT, I COMMIT TO SHOWING A LOVE THAT <u>IS CAREFUL TO HOLD THE WOUNDED AND TENDER</u>.

WHITE WOMEN + FRIENDSHIP

THIS CHAPTER MAY SOUND ODD, but these women and our friendship need a special section that speaks to the nature of cross-racial female and femme friendships. Some of these friendships, certainly the ones I hold, tackle the obstacles that actively and continually work at our racial divide, which never truly intended for us to love one another well. This culturally created chasm of race makes every effort to keep white women and women of color from any real relationship of depth and understanding. Any friendship I have with white women requires work on both our parts, work which isn't specifically necessary for relationships I have with women of color. To begin and sustain cross-racial friendships, I must acknowledge the particularity of effort and commitment we all must put forth to love each other. The three white women friendships I am sharing continue to awe me with their willingness and ability to address racism as it shows up in themselves, their families, and their communities.

A FEMINIST MORMON HOUSEWIFE

WHITE WOMEN + FRIENDSHIP

I REMEMBER MEETING LISA at Utah State University in a Women's History course (seems about right). There are some friends in this life, at least in my own life, that find you. You are not necessarily looking for a friend or friendship but these types of folks are friend finders. They notice you even if you're hiding, they see you even if you are trying to be small and invisible, and they reach out to you even if you are distant.

Lisa Butterworth found me. Lisa, with her long red hair that reached her waist, from a small Utah coal mining town, the youngest of eight children, found me, this Brooklyn-by-way-of-Brownsville, Texas-transplant Black/Brown girl. She greeted me every class. Walked with me after class. Invited me to dinner at her house. She was already married when we were becoming friends. Her husband, Nyle, has to be one of the gentlest humans I have ever met. Still is. She and Nyle graduated and moved to Idaho for their jobs. Even while she and I were apart, we held onto our friendship. In all honesty, in the early years after she moved away, Lisa held on more than I did. Distance did not deter Lisa; she wouldn't let me slip away. During those years in which I was distant and drowning in my own life, I am grateful for her persistence to pull me up and near her.

One of the ways Lisa kept me near was inviting me to go on a weekend camping trip with her, just the two of us, through Utah and Arizona. I was dubious about this adventure because I was not a person that likes to be out in the elements, nor am I still. I like nature and all, but not for too long and not too close. But Lisa promised me this would be fun. Mind you, Lisa also thought it was fun to be a fire watcher living in a small tower on top of a mountain for a whole summer by herself. So, off we went into the wild.

Our first night camping, someplace with lots of rocks and no people, I tried to help her set up the tent, but I was more of a hindrance than a help. When we finally got all settled into our sleeping bags in the dark, I asked her for a flashlight. I needed the flashlight to essentially be our night light because it was too dark out here and someone could sneak up and kill us and no one would find either of us for days. Lisa kindly reminded me that the moonlight should be light enough and that I was kinda wasting the battery but if I needed the light, it was there. I sure did need that light and it stayed on all night. Lisa was ready for sleep and was comfortably settling in when I asked why I couldn't hear anything outside. Her reply: "Isn't nice to have this silence when no one is around? It's perfect." Her idea of perfection and mine were vastly different, I told her. This was our first and last night camping in that there wilderness. The second night I pleaded for a hotel, and she obliged. Thank the good Lord for the blessing of amenities. We drove through beautiful scenic country, sang along to Tracy Chapman, and got a speeding ticket in Arizona. It was one of the best times in our friendship.

Throughout Lisa's first years living in Idaho, she spoke often of her frustration about living out her feminism within the LDS faith. She felt isolated in both her political and social views. We had many a conversation about these topics over the years and both bemoaned the struggles of living our faith and our feminism, especially in communities that largely didn't think like us. In 2004, she decided to start a blog about her stories and experiences within the church. Lisa is a writer and I fully supported anything that allowed my friend both an avenue and a reason to write. Within a few years, the blog Feminist Mormon Housewives[1] had a talented group of mostly white women writers sharing their stories. Lisa's project propelled her into a wonderful community of women all over the nation and the world. The blog was featured in the *New York Times*.[2] Its success was clearly supporting a widespread audience that needed this space, these stories, and most importantly, this community.

As Lisa dove into her newfound community of LDS women, she always and constantly invited me to write for the

---

1. feministmormonhousewives.org. Also see the book about the first ten years of the blog: *Where We Stand: The First 10 years of Feminist Mormon Housewives*, by Sara S. K. Hanks, edited by Nancy Ross.
2. Ruth Graham, "Among Mormon Women, Frank Talk About Sacred Underclothes," *New York Times*, July 21, 2021.

blog. A few times I took her up on that. She also invited me to their Facebook group. I am thankful that Lisa made every attempt to bring me along with her as she grew something very special. But I couldn't help but feel that Lisa was finding new friends and a community that understood her better than I did. Even as she invited me into her feminist circles, never leaving me out or unremembered, I did not fully feel connected to this new community. I was still a NYC Black/Brown girl, and a large group of feminist white women did not seem to reach me in the ways I needed. While it met Lisa's needs and desires for community, it did not meet my own, not without me trying. It just wasn't my community the way it was hers.

I remember the conversation we had when I finally got up enough strength to let Lisa know that I would like to gently exit the Facebook group. While I was happy for her, and I fully realized that she was making every effort to draw me in to her new beloved community (as she always did), I could not go with her. Her community of white women feminists was not a place for this Black women feminist. She understood. We may have both shed a few tears during this conversation because while she understood me and I understood her, it still hurt that we could not both find acceptance and beloved community in the same space. This sucks; the whole conversation sucked. I felt in part I was losing my friend, yet I let her know that I was holding on to her. While Lisa may have found the community she needed, I was still her community too. This turn took our friendship into another season. This time, I reached for Lisa, held her close and she let me.

LOVE SHOWED UP AS <u>AN INVITATION FOR FRIEND-SHIP</u> AND SHOWERED ME IN <u>PERSISTENCE</u>. AS A RECIPIENT OF THIS ACT OF LOVE ABUNDANT, I COMMIT TO SHOWING A LOVE THAT <u>STICKS THROUGH THE SEASONS.</u>

FURTHER + MORE:

While I was no longer part of the social media group, this small gathering of Feminist Mormon Housewives still cared for me. One year while I was in grad school, I couldn't afford coats for my children, in addition to several life happenings that were not in the budget. This group somehow found out. (I know it was Lisa who told them.) Out of the blue, they raised several hundred dollars together and sent me a cash gift. When I had my second miscarriage, one of the women called and then stopped by my house with bags (and I mean bags) of groceries and a gift card to the local grocery store. Though I quietly left the group, they turned out to be much like Lisa: they did not leave me.

BOOKWORK + TRUSTWORK

WHITE WOMEN + FRIENDSHIP

I FIRST MET MARGARET OLSEN HEMMING at an LDS women retreat, where I was asked to speak. On the flight back home from New Hampshire, we realized we were both heading home to Raleigh-Durham. We found a way to sit next to one another and talked the two-hour-long flight. On our descent, we readily made plans to meet up again.

I was in the middle of divinity school when Margaret and I started having lunch together. Each time, Margaret always managed to inquire about what I was learning in school. I readily expressed my exuberance over learning how to interpret and teach about scripture. As we continued getting to know one another, we also shared bits and pieces of our spiritual and religious journeys within the LDS religion: Margaret, a devout and active Latter-day Saint feminist, and me, not so much.

Oddly enough, while I had left the pews of the LDS church, I did not go too far. Through therapy and some rough soul work, urged on by my seminary experience, I found a peace-filled and piece-meal way to part from the church. I often describe my egress from the LDS faith as an amicable divorce. As part our divorce proceedings the church and I had what I call an ongoing custody agreement.

The LDS church and I had joint custody over the beliefs and practices they taught me that continued to breathe life into my journey with the Divine. The church, on the other hand, had sole custody of the doctrines and beliefs that did not offer me light or had ceased to serve me in my relationship with God. For instance, the LDS religion has sole custody of the idea that priesthood and ordination is gender bound to solely males. The ideas around service and taking care of one another, now that — *that* — I took with me. I held on to the parts of the faith that still sung to me, offered me a greater glimpse of God, and continued to feed my spirit well.

To me, the Book of Mormon was one of those lovely LDS keepsakes. I am not stingy with scripture. In fact, I hold the definition of scripture with a freedom and flexibility. I work to refrain my personal notions that holy text can only come through a certain people in a certain time and place. So, when Margaret suggested that we partner together to write a commentary for the Book of Mormon from a social justice lens, I was both excited and reluctant. As an editor and a writer herself, Margaret felt that my ideas about the Book of Mormon should be written. I did not have time to write anything outside the required papers for my coursework. So my immediate answer was a firm no. There was no time. Margaret then devised a plan where we would meet, I would talk about the text in conversation with her, she would record it, then transcribe it. At first, it seemed doable. So, I hesitantly agreed.

We started meeting weekly and recording our conversations. Soon it became time to have a talk about authorship. This was a rough conversation. I did not trust Margaret enough to think that she wouldn't try to take ownership of work that wasn't solely hers. In fact, I backed away from the project until we could decide how we were going to rightly name our parts in this project. It took us some time, some tears, and a lot of conversation over the historical nature of Black work and white theft. In the beginning, I didn't feel I could readily trust her; it was a trust that needed to be built. She too had hesitations about writing the book with me if she did not get any acknowledgement for her part. We also had to confront the historical nature of a woman's work and skills not being valued or seen, regardless of any race or ethnicity. So, we found ourselves at an impasse.

We had a series of hard conversations and then decided to halt the project for some time while we figured out how to do our partnership well. I convened my love circle, spoke with them at length, I prayed and fasted. After some time, I asked Margaret if we could have shared billing, but with a verbiage that allowed for the complexity of this partnership. The first volume of *The Book of Mormon for the Least of These* reads: Fatimah Salleh *with* Margaret Olsen Hemming. We both detailed our process in the preface. By the second volume of the book, Margaret and I were coauthors: Fatimah Salleh *and* Margaret Olsen Hemming. The third and final volume, soon to come out as of this writing, will again have both of us as authors. While I still had a part in the book, it was mostly Margaret. It was my suggestion that she take sole billing. She immediately refused and fervently fought against it, so once again we are co-authors.

In the beginning I reserved my trust. In the preface of the second volume, I wrote about Margaret and our friendship, her brilliance, and work ethic. Years later, through all the work and conversations, that trust is intentionally and freely offered. Margaret and I did not just build a working relationship; we built a friendship.

LOVE SHOWED UP AS <u>A TRUST TO BE BUILT</u> AND SHOWERED ME IN <u>AN EVOLUTION OF FRIENDSHIP.</u> AS A RECIPIENT OF THIS ACT OF LOVE ABUNDANT, I COMMIT TO SHOWING A LOVE THAT <u>WORKS TO DEFY HISTORY'S RACIAL CHASMS.</u>

FURTHER + MORE:

Margaret recently decided to apply to Duke Divinity School for her second master's degree. Her first was from American University in Peace and Conflict Studies. I could not be more thrilled when she asked me to write her a letter of recommendation. Recently she was accepted, and she immediately called me to celebrate. I am excited for her. As I wrote in my letter of recommendation, "Duke Divinity School will be a better place because Margaret is there."

ORGANIZED REBELLION
WHITE WOMEN + FRIENDSHIP

CASEY STANTON AND I WERE BOTH NURSING mothers when we started seminary together in 2013. As fate and God would have it, we were both in the same Spiritual Formation class with Rev. Liz Dowling-Sendor. Casey, a Catholic from Boston with an Italian mother and a Jewish father, had enough energy and volume to let you know she had entered a room. It made sense that before divinity school, she was a community organizer.

Casey and I connected from the get-go. We were both mothers and older than most of the students. Even fewer were nursing mamas. Although we were both married and juggling babies, Casey was far more involved in the happenings of the school than I was. She hosted poetry nights and dinners for our seminary community, while I generally stayed at home trying to wrangle four children. Her home became a place where our group of classmates could routinely find a warm welcome and good food.

The world continued spinning outside our seminary enclave. On August 9, 2014, Michael Brown was murdered by a police officer in Ferguson, Missouri. In the months following his death, the nation erupted into protests at yet another Black person dying at the hands of local police. As

Ferguson became a hotbed of Black Lives Matter protests that started to sweep the nation, I fell into a deep sadness laced with rage. I had hard discussions with my three sons and daughter. With each publicized murder of an unarmed Black person, I took my children aside and had the same dreaded ongoing conversation, allowing them to mourn and make space for the spectrum of emotions. Then I would urge them to be safe, to take precautions. I let my heart hold onto them in a world that hunted them.

One of the days following Brown's death, my friend Casey approached me at school enraged and ready. "Fatimah, this is all so awful. What are we going to do?" she asked.

"*We*, Casey? I am not going to do anything right now besides what I am already doing."

She replied, "The divinity school doesn't seem to be doing anything or saying anything about this. Christ would not be silent. I want to plan a worship service. I am going to try to reserve the chapel and lay out a program. Will you help me plan it?"

"I don't know, Casey."

"Just think about it and pray about it, please?" That is always dangerous when someone asks you to pray about something. Casey is notorious for asking me to pray and follow the Spirit. It's also why I try to hedge off any plans she might have early on in our conversations, because I now suspect where it may be headed and I ain't praying about no more work to do. I let Casey know that I would pray and think about joining her. Meanwhile, Casey went right along moving in her plans as if my answer was already a yes. (Friends should not let friends have organizers as friends.)

Casey then pitched her idea, with me in tow, to Rev. Dr. Eboni Marshall-Turman, the Director of The Office of Black Church Studies at Duke Divinity. Coincidentally, she was also teaching our Black Theology course at the time. Dr. Marshall-Turman heard us out (well, mainly Casey), gave us her support, and encouraged this service to be completely student-led. We were, in fact, hoping that she would preach at the service and invited her to do so, despite her counsel for it to be student-led. She quickly turned the tables and looked directly at me. "Why don't you preach, Fatimah?"

"What?! No. We were hoping you, or if not you, one of the faculty here would preach into this moment."

"And what would make you less able to preach into this moment, Fatimah?"

"I don't know…" I stammered. "I just don't feel comfortable."

"Well, think about it. Give it some prayer," she prompted.

Meanwhile, Casey was looking at me with that cheesy grin of hers. As we walked out of Dr. Marshall-Turman's office, Casey enthusiastically continued to talk to me about the program and casually named me as the preacher of the hour as if it was already a done deal.

Her/our plans did not go unnoticed. The dean of the divinity school did not take it well that we were planning this service without his oversight, which we didn't know we needed. Adding insult to injury, he was also upset that we had not invited him to take part in the service that was now being widely publicized throughout the school and our local community. After a confrontation of sorts with the school's chaplain, where the dean's dismay was relayed, we readily decided that the dean would offer the benediction. Powers now somewhat appeased, we kept planning.

I went on, worried and apprehensive about the whole service. One of my friends and fellow classmates warned that she did not want the service to be a place where white people could once again be voyeurs to our grief. I immediately brought this concern to Casey and began to back out of the planning. I did not want to do anything that would further harm my folks. Perhaps an interracial, intercultural worship space was not what we, as Black people, needed. Days before the program, I was still doubting my part in the program. Even more I doubted I could deliver any sermon at this time. I just could not see God in all of this. I did not know how to preach from this moment, despite Dr. Eboni Marshall-Turman's prompting.

A few days before the service, I had so many doubts, and Casey showed up at what seemed like the middle of the night at my doorstep. We had just gotten off the phone and I expressed my deep desire to withdraw from it all. Someone else could preach. Someone else could help with the last details of the program. I wanted out. We hung up the phone with each other, only for Casey to appear at my door minutes later. Right there at my doorstep, under my front porch light. Alarmed, I asked her what she was doing running around at night and knocking on people's doors.

"This conversation could not happen over the phone, so I came to say this in person. There is so much heartbreak in our world. I know very well I might get this wrong, but I would rather try and learn from my mistakes than do nothing and say nothing at all. I will continue to pray we do no harm and that as a minimum we provide the space for Jesus to enter and speak. Please don't back out."

Tears rolling down my face, I hugged her and relented. "I'm in. I pray we get this as right as we can; my people do not need any more harm."

Now I had to wrestle with my sermon. There was no backing out now; I had just given my word to deliver the Word. Yet I found myself without any words, just a fury. A fury at God for what I saw as failing Black people repeatedly for so long. How could I utter any semblance of a faithful sermon when I felt so disappointed in the Divine? Where was God for Black people?

So, I went to the only person I knew who could answer my question. I went to my Nana. I practically screeched as I asked her how she could continue to worship and pray to a God that did not seem to answer in the way our people needed God. My Nana was quiet and listened to my loud lament. And then she asked me, "Who you got, Timah? You got anyone better than my God?"

I paused for a long while and sighed, "No, Nana. I don't."

"Then, I am going to keep worshipping and praying to my God. You let me know if you got anyone better."

And that's how I began my sermon. Not in the knowing of God but in the unknowing and the faithfulness of my Nana's questions.

News outlets showed up. The chapel was packed. Nana sat in the front. Casey walked the back seeing that everything ran smoothly and according to plan.[1]

LOVE SHOWED UP AS <u>A FRIEND'S PUSH</u> AND SHOWERED ME IN <u>THE POWER OF ORGANIZING.</u> AS A RECIPIENT OF THIS ACT OF LOVE ABUNDANT, I COMMIT TO SHOWING A LOVE THAT <u>ALLOWS FRIENDS TO NUDGE ME TO ACTION.</u>

---

1. Watch the whole service: "Litany, Lament and Liberation," Dec 12, 2014, youtube.com/watch?v=8bBzQa4w5r0

COME OUT AND STAY IN

ARA SERJOIE AND I MET MY JUNIOR YEAR at Utah State University. He actually has a vivid memory of how we first met but that's not how I remember it. Since I am doing the writing, I refrain from relaying his first impression of me. Regardless of that initial encounter of which I bear little to no memory, we became good friends. We were such good friends that I asked him to be my campaign manager when I ran for student body president at USU. I personally think Ara reveled in ordering me around and telling me what to do for several weeks.

When I got married, Ara arrived a day early for the wedding. When touring our venue, Ara decided that we needed floral centerpieces for the pavilion's wood picnic tables. I rolled my eyes. We were in the middle of the forest, foliage was everywhere, we did not need more. Ara strongly disagreed. After our rehearsal, he proceeded to draft me and part of the wedding party to search the surrounding area for flowers and such so he could assemble centerpieces for each table. While we all foraged the forest, we mumbled about Ara's need to have more flowers and how just 24 hours before the wedding we were all out here collecting greenery. Undaunted by our complaints, Ara worked his magic, making us all stay another hour to finish the final details and voila! Gorgeous natural centerpieces graced the rustic tables. After our grumbling, we thanked him.

After graduation, Ara lived about an hour and a half away from my family. He regularly traveled to have dinner with all of us. Our family began to think of him as family and still do.

One day, out of the blue it seemed, Ara asked me to lunch because he wanted to have a talk with me. We met at a restaurant and after catching up on our lives, laughing per usual at life's happenings, he took a long pause. "I guess you're wondering what I wanted to talk about."

"You're gay," I said.

Surprised Ara replied, "Well, yeah…how did you know?"

"I don't know. You usually tell me a lot about your life, this seemed serious and there was a fairly big build up, so I guessed. But I should have let you say it. I am sorry."

"No, you're ok. Are you upset? What are you thinking?" I can see why this would be the big questions. My friend was coming out to me, a devout Mormon at the time, whose religion expressly denounced homosexuality. Yet I could not find it in me to think differently of my longtime friend.

"I love you, Ara. Nothing is going to change that. Let's eat some lunch and you can tell me if you're dating anyone!"

"Yes, let's," he replied. Ara, the godfather of my eldest son, is now married to a wonderful man and I am grateful that he loved me enough and found me a safe enough space, despite my religious beliefs, that he would risk sharing his full self with me.

Since this day, I have had several beautiful friends trust me with some of their first talks about their truths. I am always humbled and find myself celebrating them and their pronouncements of self. For they are to be celebrated, held, and honored. Ara was the first to love me in a way that asked me to see more of him, the whole of him.

LOVE SHOWED UP AS <u>TRUTH SHARING</u> AND SHOWERED ME IN <u>A RISKY TRUST.</u> AS A RECIPIENT OF THIS ACT OF LOVE ABUNDANT, I COMMIT TO SHOWING A LOVE THAT IS <u>WORTHY OF THE RISK AND THE TRUST.</u>

LOVE CIRCLE ROLL CALL

MY "LOVE CIRCLE." That's what I have named those whom I love and love me.

Some time ago, I overheard my sons analyzing the success of the San Antonio Spurs, the NBA basketball team. "Well, you know why they had such a winning streak…it's because of their deep bench," they chattered.

"What is a deep bench?" I interrupted.

"It's when your second string of players, those on the bench, are just as good as your first string," they explained.

It hit me that while I had a tight love circle, it would be, at times, unfair to ask any one person to be what I needed all the time. I started to pray for a love circle with a "deep bench." I prayed that I would recognize and find people whom I could love and who could love me well. And God blew my mind. I started to cultivate and truly see the depth of my love circle. Some folks in my love circle share little to none of my religious beliefs; some are in the LGBQTIA+ community; others span racial and ethnic backgrounds; my elders and the younger generation…they are nothing short of an assembly of God's good creations. In awe of their spectacular selves, I decided to share some of the characteristics and attributes of the people in my love circle. I would not want to do life without folks like this in my home, on the phone, in my worship spaces, and in the world.

FAITHFUL FAMILY
LOVE CIRCLE ROLL CALL

AS THE ELDEST OF SEVEN, I look back and describe myself as a soft tyrant over my siblings. We were a single parent home where I was often left in charge. I am sure my siblings have no shortage of tales to describe my time at the helm. Through our growing years we all attended church together. Today, as adults, we encompass a wide spectrum of beliefs between the seven of us, everything from a reverend (me) to agnostics and off/on atheists.

Yet, despite or perhaps even with our disparate beliefs, in every milestone I experienced in religious spaces, my siblings have rejoiced and celebrated with me. When I wrote a book about Latter-day Saint scripture, they bought it — with no intention of reading it. When I preached, no matter the religious venue, they showed up, many of my siblings living in another state. I tried to figure out how my siblings manage to sit in places where they share little in common with the community, but I gave that up and accepted that it did not matter — they were there for me, and I could not be more grateful.

When I had to give my first eulogy at a funeral, my sister Kalilah asked me if I needed her there. I didn't, really, but she was willing to be at my side.

My siblings taught me that you do not have to share the same beliefs or lifestyle to show up in love. I hope we all can get family, chosen or otherwise, who choose to show up for us.

GET YOU SOME FOLKS IN YOUR LOVE CIRCLE THAT WILL SHOW UP FOR YOU. FROM THEM I HAVE LEARNED TO SHOW UP FOR OTHERS IN SPACES THAT ARE NOT NECESSARILY MY OWN.

LAUGHTER
LOVE CIRCLE ROLL CALL

MY FRIEND, VIVETTE JEFFERIES-LOGAN, calls laughter "good medicine." One of the ways I promised I would be gentler with myself was to try to find laughter daily. I encounter so much humor talking with the witty and lively folks in my community. I also find that I can laugh at myself because I am definitely a work in process and sometimes just a plain hot mess.

Over the years, I paid close attention to humor and how it impacts my life. For example, one of the reasons I am still married to Eric is because he is so damn funny. I have never known a human to get me so angry, until our four children. Together 23+ years and he can get on my nerves like no one else. I often tell him that I was a nice person before I was married and had children.

One time, I got so upset at Eric, that during our argument I swear my voice dropped an octave and I was suddenly, a baritone. Surprised at my new enraged vocal prowess, I took myself to the living room to take some deep breaths. Moments later, I found a note on our bedroom door with a hand drawn cross and an actual garlic clove attached to it. The note on the door insinuated that I had turned into a vampire, and this would protect my husband and children.

I laughed so hard as I reread the note and held the piece of garlic in my hand. I do not know how Eric does it, but he does. His humor has a way of dissolving so much of my frustrations. While Eric is handsome, that only goes so far with me — but his humor, his ability to make me laugh at the mundane and the dramatic, makes life so much more doable.

I don't know if it is because we grew up in the same household, but my siblings and I share the same familial humor. Our family text threads, which occur every once in a while (because fights have broken out for less), still remain one of the funniest places I find myself. I mean, who can forget how my brother, Asaad, went through a period as a teenager when he hid in strange places and lurked around corners just to scare the hell out of us. He went as far as to lock himself away in cabinets, stand behind shower curtains, lay in the back seat of the car, and jump out from behind the mailbox just to hear us all scream. He literally had our whole family shook for months. More than these memories we share in laughter, my family has a wit I get. It is nothing for me to call them when life gets hard and find I am laughing through my tears. If my family had a superpower this would be one.

My children are not far behind in offering me plenty of fodder for laughter. Whether it's the antics of their youth or their constant test trials of their wit, they offer me many memories of laughter. Some love memories of laughter that still make me giggle:

When I asked my 3-year-old Ronin why he was not dressed and he simply replied, "I am. I have my penis on."

After tutoring, 10-year-old Zora stated, "I wish math would grow up and solve its own problems. I am not a therapist."

Or Micah, then a 5th grader, conscripted Xavier, a 3rd grader, to write his letter of apology to his teacher. The letter written in great penmanship, misspelled "posotive" but was definitely signed "From Micah" — in Xavier's handwriting.

How Ronin ran into our bedroom and told us he tore his hamstring and therefore couldn't go to school.

When Xavier would only wear superhero costumes and the neighbors didn't think he owned any other clothing.

Micah and Xavier developed a game where they would stomp on each other's shadows, better known as "shadow stomping." Almost always this violent game of shadows erupted into yelling and tears. I find myself laughing now remembering my admonishments, "Leave each other shadows alone! Stop stomping on his shadow!"

The stories are endless...

GET YOURSELF SOME FUNNY FOLKS IN YOUR LOVE CIRCLE, SO THAT THEIR "GOOD MEDICINE" CAN OFFER YOU HEALING.

ANGER BEARERS
LOVE CIRCLE ROLL CALL

ANGER BEARERS ARE THE BEST. These are the folks in your love circle that get angry on your behalf. They are fiercely protective of you and have no problem coming to your defense. They are not necessarily cool-headed; in fact, their love for you is in touch with their rage. I often describe anger as a forest fire, and anger bearers as the controlled burn set by firefighters to meet and offset an uncontrolled blaze.[1]

My husband Eric is one of the best anger bearers. This man is so in touch with his anger. Part of his white male privilege is that white masculine roles allow for their anger. As a Black/Brown woman there is a prevailing and insidious trope attached to my anger, whereas that is not the societal stereotype placed on my husband. Yet Eric is particularly skilled, having honed his anger on my behalf. Eric already had an attachment to certain curse words by the time he was five years old. Years of working on construction sites and living in New York did little to abate his fluency in foul language. Our first years of marriage, I would cringe at his word choice. Now, oddly enough, I come to expect

---

1. This is the origin of the phrase "Fight fire with fire." Read more at "Why Firefighters Set Backfires: The Science of Controlled Burns" at firefighterinsider.com.

his cursing and often look for it when I tell him about any given incident. His cursing and instant anger for me, is, in part, cathartic. Where I try to squelch my hurt and ensuing anger, Eric gives a whole clearing for the burn.

Once I told him about a conversation I had with a Duke Divinity administrator who found out I was leaving my position as an academic assistant director at the school. They told me that I would never make the money I was receiving at my current position by starting my own business as a consultant.[2] This administrator then went on to ask me what my husband did for a job, then said, "Well, at least with your husband, your kids won't starve."

I called Eric and his first words were, "F*$& him! We don't give an eff what he thinks. You have never needed the word of any man, certainly not this [insert another curse word]! Don't you listen to him, Timah. You want me to go over there and talk with him? Because you know I will." Through my frustrated tears, I smiled. "No, Eric, there's no need to talk to him." I smiled again. Then I had the pleasure of listening to him rant in all his colorful language about how men think they can just go around pooping on folks' dreams. I almost wish I could record his diatribes; they are truly a work of verbal art, yet not for the faint of heart.

Another anger bearer in my life is my sister Kalilah. I wrote a Facebook post a few years ago about my experience

---

2. See ACertainWork.org for details about workshops & training, consulting & curriculum development, and speaking & engaging, and Curanopy Ministries, a religious non-profit that focuses on clergy wellness and wellbeing.

joining my son for his two days of ISS (in-school suspension).[3] My post went viral and with that came an onslaught of public support as well as public venom. The comments attacked my motherhood and my child. I do not think I was ready for that kind of vitriol and decided to stop reading the comments early on, per the advice of my love circle. My sister, on the other hand, told me simply that she had time and a keyboard, and asked if I would give her permission to respond. "Sure, I am not looking at those comments anymore. My spirit can't take it."

"I got you," she said.

Next thing I knew she was handing out truth with a serving of "leave my sister alone," complete with memes and GIFs. Since I turned off my notifications, the family text feed was where I heard the latest in her social media slaughter. In the wake of racist, ignorant, and hurtful comments, my sister ran a single-woman response campaign.

While I talk about Eric and Kalilah, that is not to say that there are not others in my love circle who do not hold this same gift. I remember calling a friend of mine, twice in a row by accident, and her text back read, "I am in a meeting, but do I need to leave and take off my earrings to fight somebody?"

And never forget our mamas. My mama took a day off work, drove to my college, and demanded to speak to the

---

3. I originally joined my son in ISS because I wanted to make sure he wasn't given more time in ISS because of his jocular behavior. I also accompanied him, in part, because I didn't believe the conditions were as bad as he described.

Vice President to handle an incident with me and another undergraduate. There was no stopping her, despite me saying I was gonna be okay.

Thank God for anger bearers, the controlled burn that assuages my fire. It is a good place where one's anger can be met with a glorious indignation that alleviates the burden of the hurt.

GET YOURSELF SOME ANGER BEARERS IN YOUR LOVE CIRCLE SO THAT YOU DO NOT HAVE TO HOLD IT ALONE. FROM MY ANGER BEARERS I LEARN TO SHARE IN THE RAGE.

THE *WHOOP!* WING OF THE LOVE CIRCLE

LOVE CIRCLE ROLL CALL

WHILE DISCUSSING YET ANOTHER one of my harebrained ideas with my husband, he listened and then abruptly declared, "You know, if you told me you wanted to start a worm farm for Jesus, I would grab a bucket, a small shovel, and ask, 'Where should we start digging?'" I laughed and looked at him to find out if he was serious. "I mean it. I trust your ideas and vision," he told me.

The funny part was that I did not trust my ideas and vision. I did not understand how Eric always seemed to affirm my quirkiest idea, and not only affirm it but be excited for me to try. My sister, Najah, told me that she first went to Eric for all her ideas because he never said no and always saw possibility. Eric has a knack for heartily encouraging the absurd, the risky, and the creative.

For example, I did not find out until years later that he didn't think my going back to school to pursue a master's of divinity was a great idea. He simply said, "I really didn't see what that degree would give you that the PhD didn't, but I have learned to trust you and your inclinations. I am glad now that I didn't voice my hesitations because I would have been wrong. It turned out to be something you really needed." That's Eric. He reserves his reservations and leans heavily into offering encouragement and support.

Maybelline Alvarez McCoy, my Afro-Panamanian friend and sister, bounces up and down with excitement for me when I bring her my ideas, acting downright giddy. "Amor, si!" she shouts, "What can I do? You know I will do everything I can to help on my end. Tell me where and when you need me." After a lengthy rallying session, Maybelline starts connecting the dots of my vision and offers to put me in contact with others who can help add clarity, resources, and wisdom to my idea. She actually takes me through a lovely process:

1. celebration of the idea and of me,
2. more celebration,
3. an honest offering of support, and
4. an invitation to connect with people who can walk with me.

There is also Elena Montano-Rock, who shows up as a quiet and reserved *whoop*!

When I said I was leaving the LDS church, Elena said, "Let me know where you go and I will support you in every way I can from across the country."

When I said I wanted to write a book, she said, "I have some money saved and I would like to buy you a ticket to Arizona for a few days so that you have the quiet and time to write."

And when I say, "I don't think I can do what God wants me to do," she says, "Sure, you can."

She checks in and frequently asks, "when and where are you preaching next?" (I don't usually tell folks and she knows that.) Then she tunes in, listens and always sends me a message, affirming me. Always affirming me from across the country, in a different time zone and miles away. Elena is the quiet *whoop!* of presence and prayer.

I am grateful for the love that shows up as the enthusiastic and heartfelt *whoop!* — the enthusiastic encouragement that celebrates with and for you.

GET YOU A *WHOOP!* WING OF YOUR LOVE CIRCLE. LET THEM CHEER YOU ON AS YOU DISCOVER HOW POWERFUL YOU ARE. FROM MY *WHOOP!* WING, I LEARNED TO CELEBRATE ZANY AND BOLD IDEAS.

GRIEF WALKERS
LOVE CIRCLE ROLL CALL

REV. DR. KATHY DUNTON and Rev. Bernadine Anthony ("Bernie") and I all knew each other before we were reverends. We met at Duke Divinity School in one fateful class that shall go unnamed. It was a required course, and the material was being taught in such a way that I had long given up hope of doing well in the class. I just needed a C to graduate. Bernie, also struggling, decided to take matters into her own hands and recruit a study group. It just so happens that she created a study group with four people who all were lost. Besides us three Black women, we had one other member of our group, Keith, a white man who snuck in and ended up being a beloved presence. That's after we told him to not touch Black women's hair; two years later he told us he was thankful for the advice.

It was in that there crucible of a class that Bernie, Kathy, and I began our longtime friendship. We grappled all semester long, meeting often to get a handle on our graded material. In between memorizing the long list of Christian crusades and other religious debauchery, we started to get to know one another and share our lives outside of that study space. We graduated in succession and remained intentional about staying close afterwards.

We found each other amid the COVID-19 pandemic when we all experienced so much loss. Bernie and I were with Kathy when she lost her nephew in a car accident. Kathy and I were there when Bernie lost her father. And they both were there when I lost my grandmother and auntie. These are the women who let me fall apart. Women have held me when I felt like I did not know if I had enough faith to keep on believing. They let me question God, lose my faith, and find it again. We know each other's families and our families know one another.

When Lucy, our doggy of nine years, passed away in 2021, our family was devastated. I called Bernie and Kathy and just wept. I confessed that it felt weird to weep so hard over a pet during so much human devastation. Yet they reassured me that this too was a grief that should not be understated. A few weeks after Lucy's death, Bernie and Kathy said they had bought a gift for our family: an hourlong session with a pet medium, a person who was said to talk to animals who have passed on. Bernie and Kathy had been talking, and even though they had never been to a pet medium, they had heard great things about this one.

I was shocked. I asked them if they thought it could be possible, this pet medium. "We don't know but we also don't limit what God can do and it may give you the goodbye y'all need. We are hoping in that. We are also actually praying really hard this works out," they confessed.

I took some time and delayed contacting the pet medium for several weeks, unsure of it all. I talked to our family and they were all just as unsure as I was, but the kiddos were far more willing to give it a try. The day came to speak with the medium. We all sat around, weary and dubious. When I tell you that this woman had us all in tears, captivated by what she was saying to us about Lucy, I tell our truth. She relayed things only we knew as a family. When the hour session ended, we all sat there looking at each other, dumbfounded and smiling through the tears. As he was leaving the living room, Micah said, "What would ever make your two clergy friends give us something like this? It was the best gift. They are goated[1] in my book." The rest of the children wholeheartedly agreed and asked me to thank my friends profusely.

When I called Kathy and Bernie to offer our collective gratefulness, they simultaneously exhaled. "Ohhh, we were worried about this. We are so thankful it turned out to be a good experience for the family." And we all laughed. I knew they were just as nervous as we were, entering this unknown.

While our friendship has seen each other through grief and loss, we have also taken every opportunity to celebrate each other. It is not just that these women can walk with me in grief and entertain wild notions of care; they are women who practice a style of presence that holds one well.

---

1. Gen Z slang for GOAT, Greatest Of All Time.

GET YOURSELF FOLKS THAT LET YOU FALL APART
AND TEACH YOU THE DIVINE ART OF PRESENCE.

LOVE SHOWED UP AS <u>A MYRIAD OF LOVED ONES</u>
AND SHOWERED ME IN <u>THEIR GIFTS AND POWER.</u>
AS A RECIPIENT OF THIS ACT OF LOVE ABUNDANT, I
COMMIT TO <u>BEING AN AUTHENTIC FORCE OF LOVE.</u>

A CONTINUATION, NOT A CONCLUSION...

I THOUGHT ABOUT HOW TO END THIS BOOK but how does one begin to end a book about love memories? Even as I write, more memories keep surfacing, and even more memories are being made. There is no ending to this work, just a soft and grace-filled continuation. An ellipsis. A "to be continued." As for me, I think my holy hush is coming to an end but that doesn't mean I don't intend to return to this practice when the Spirit calls me back to the quiet.

I wrote this book because I needed to remember. I felt that for me to continue in my call, I had to follow the spiritual nudging to recall and record. To do the work of love memory allows me to sink into all the ways love has been oh, so right and overflowing. Sure, there are ways that love has been less than great, but this book right here is about remembering and reminiscing the great and the more than good.

I am humbled to offer some of my memories to you. I hope some of my love work will call to your own love memories. I pray you find time to memoryscape with the beloveds in your life.

As part of this continuation, I hope you allow me to offer a few blessings in love:

Back
may you find the memories that take you
back.
back to moments, times, days, and epochs of love abundant.
back
to the taste of love on your tongue
back
to the loves that urge you to face forward
back
to when you were jelly in the embrace of another
may you go back and find yourself all wrapped in love

part for you
may time part for you
so you can remember
perhaps with another
or just you and spirit
may time make way for your memories
may the parting of time put you together again

mouth open
oh may love memories find you with your mouth open
open to giggles,
the hearty guffaws,
the belly aches of laughter,
and yes, even the snorts
oh, may your heart and mouth be open to meet
in rhythm and riff with one another
mouth wide open with the sounds of hilarity in love

let love
letting love teach you
hold you
follow you
go before and beside you
whisper sweet somethings
love let the divinity in you and another come forth
let love
do its thing
letting love be a witness and a testimony
letting love
be a baby and an elder
we let love move wild as we run alongside
Let love.

AFTERWORD

This book is merely an offering.

My musings in memories of love abundant is my offering.

I have to say that I am sad to see this book end. The process of remembering love in all its myriad of manifestations has offered me such spiritual nourishment. The memory work required to write these stories has fed me. Not just a high caloric intake with low nutritional value. No, this was nutrient-dense soul work and I am better for it.

I told my kiddos that if only one family member reads this book, it has already been worth the journey. Writing these love memories freed me in some ways. Certainly, while the love I have received came to me in abundance, I know God asks a price: to offer unto others what has been wondrously offered to me. I circle back to Luke 12:48: "Where much is given, much is required." I do not think I had the depth of understanding (probably still don't) of what love has given me until I started remembering.

I am grateful to all the good folks who let me put their name in print and tell our love story.

I am thankful to Marci McPhee, editor extraordinaire. I handed her mushy stories and she worked to clean them up yet make sure the mushy nature of my writing voice was still present. Every edit she returned was laced with encouragement and I could not be more thankful for her kindness in correction.

Last but certainly, not least, my beloved community. They continue to love on me, creating new and newer love memories.

For certainly this work is ongoing and that's certainly the good news.

ABOUT THE AUTHOR

REV. DR. FATIMAH S. SALLEH was born in Brooklyn, New York to a Puerto-Rican and Malaysian mother and an African-American father. Dr. Salleh received her PhD in Mass Communication from the University of North Carolina at Chapel Hill. She also earned a Master's degree from Syracuse University in Public Communication and a Master of Divinity from Duke University. She launched A Certain Work in 2018 to provide racial equity consultation and training for organizations and churches. In 2021, Curanopy Ministries, a religious non-profit, was established to focus on clergy wellness and wellbeing. Both organizations, A Certain Work and Curanopy Ministries, are built upon a lasting commitment to equity, justice, and grace by being in "right relationship" with one another.

ACW

Made in the USA
Middletown, DE
15 March 2024